THE OTHER PLACE

Carol Arnall

Copyright © 2011 C. A. Arnall

www.carolarnall.com

All rights reserved.

All the characters are fictitious. This is a work of fiction and in no way an historical work.

No part of this work can be copied or stored in a retrieval system unless permission is obtained in writing from the publisher or author.

Cover Photograph copyright Carol Arnall 2011

ACKNOWLEDGEMENTS

Special thanks go to Hazel, the best friend in the world.

Also to my good friend, Colin Gooch, for all the information about Tamworth. Thanks, Col. A true friend, where would I be without your help?

Dedicated to
Hazel & Colin

OTHER BOOKS BY THE AUTHOR

Fiction
Dancing with Spirits
Spirits of the Lights

Non Fiction
Birmingham Girls
Mysterious Happenings
Choosing Your Psychic Pathway
Ghosts, Angels & Hauntings
Memories

www.carolarnall.com

The Other Place

Chrissie James is a troubled soul; with family problems, unexplained phobias and a stalker to contend with, she seeks help from a hypnotherapist and discovers she has led a past life.

Will living a previous life help Chrissie to discover the truth of what caused her fears and phobias, and will she find out who is stalking her?

The Other Place is a paranormal mystery. Its many twists and turns will keep you guessing to the very end.

The Other Place

CHAPTER 1

'Oh, my bum feels so cold on this step, sis; I'll have to move or I'll freeze me knickers off.'

Jumping up, twelve-year-old Chrissie James started running up and down the garden path, rubbing her backside to aid the circulation. Babs, her fourteen-year-old sister, doubled up laughing as she watched her antics. She called, 'Pack it up or you'll have the whole terrace laffing at you. Our mom will clip your ear'ole for showing us up if you ain't careful. Mind the cat, you nearly tripped over 'er, 'er'll be having 'er kittens soon, look at the size of 'er!'

Chrissie stopped dead; no way did she want to anger her mother. Their mom was someone to be reckoned with when she lost her temper.

Hearing footsteps coming up the path running between the back-to-back houses, they saw a tall, heavily built woman advancing towards their gate. She had long black hair held back with hairgrips on either side of her face. What drew Babs' attention more than anything was the slash of bright red lipstick the woman was wearing, giving her long, pale face a ghoulish look. Her blue eyes almost popping out of her head, Babs gave the woman a hard stare, which the woman returned with a wide smile, revealing the largest set of teeth the young girl had ever seen, and to make matters worse, they were smeared with lipstick. Babs froze for a minute then hurried back to her sister. Snuggling up beside

The Other Place

Chrissie on the doorstep, the girls watched the woman push the gate open and proceed to walk up the path.

'What's up, Babs?' Chrissie queried, wondering at her sister's reaction to the stranger.

'I don't like the look of 'er, Chris. She gives me the creeps.'

By this time the woman had reached them. 'Your ma in?' she demanded sharply in a strange-sounding accent.

They nodded, staring up at the woman's mouth; the girls couldn't take their eyes off her. 'Tell 'er I'm 'ere, then,' the woman demanded impatiently. 'I ain't got all day, you know.'

Clutching her sister tightly, Babs yelled, 'Mom, there's a woman 'ere wants to see you.'

'What now,' a tired-sounding voice called irritably from the darkness within. 'What ya been up to, our Babs?'

'Nuffink, Mom, an' that's the truth,' Babs shrieked. 'Ain't dun nuffink, nor our Chrissie, honestly. This 'ere woman wants to see ya. Can she come in?'

'I'm feeding ya brother. Bring her in for Gawd's sake, then go to the corner shop for me. We need some bread.'

Leaping up, Babs motioned the woman into the small dark room.

Blinking her coal-black eyes, the woman tried to adjust to the gloom. She saw a slim, blonde-haired woman feeding a baby boy of some eleven months with mashed potato, carrot and milk from a chipped cream-coloured crock dish. Two old

The Other Place

horsehair chairs in front of the fire had bits of fabric hanging in shreds beneath them. The pegged rug spread across the hearth in-between the chairs had seen better days. However, as her eyes adjusted to the gloom, she couldn't fault the young woman's housekeeping skills; she was impressed by the cleanliness of the room. The room smelt of carbolic soap and Mansion Polish. She also noticed how sparkling clean the sash window was. This really surprised her as most of the houses up the terrace had rags and newspapers plugging up broken window panes. The smoke produced by the coal fire normally put layers of dust over everything in sight, and to see such a clean room in one of these houses was astonishing. She had been expecting a drab, run-down, dirty house, but instead she noticed that even the towelling nappies airing on the fireguard gleamed white through the gloom. The flypaper hanging from the ceiling looked as if it was changed regularly, astonishing her, as normally they were a revolting sight full to overflowing with dead flies.

'Who are you and what do you want?' Lily asked the woman directly, eyeing her up and down as she busily tried to keep up with the baby's demand for his dinner.

'I'm a friend of your ex-husband, he sent me to see ya, missus,' she replied.

'Ya what?' the mother shrieked. 'Him who I divorced some years ago for adultery and desertion?'

'Er, yes, Missus?' Pausing on a stutter and stepping back, the woman licked her bright red lips nervously seeing the angry glint in Lily's green eyes.

Slamming the spoon down angrily, adding yet another crack to the already chipped dish, the young woman clasped the baby to her chest as she demanded, 'What the devil do you want? I finished with that cheat years ago. I told him I never wanted to see or hear from him again.'

'Erm,' backing towards the door the woman gabbled, 'he told me to tell you he's willing to have the girls, missus, he says he'll tek em off your 'ands. He has his own place down south, and if you like, they can come back with me.'

Her words were greeted with an almighty shriek. 'Get out of here before I brain you. The ansa's no, and don't come anywhere near us again, and you can pass the message on to 'im, as well.'

The new arrival practically ran from the room, jumping down the step and almost knocking the sisters over in her haste to escape. They heard the gate slam and the woman's high heels tip-tapping down the paved path that ran between the houses.

'Lily, Lily, my luv, are you okay?' Nellie Garden, who lived across the way, came running into the front room. Nellie was a mother of six, aged between three months and seven years, and despite her surname she wouldn't know a flower from a weed. 'I 'eard enough to know ya must be very upset by all this, me babby.'

Nothing in the terrace could be kept secret. Whatever happened inside or outside the houses would be overheard and passed along the jungle telegraph within seconds.

Lily held baby Gregory tightly in her arms.

The Other Place

'How dare he!' she exclaimed in righteous anger. 'The lying, cheating, no-good, deserting, yellow-bellied coward, how could he?' Then, bursting into tears, she sobbed, 'He wants to take me girls from me, Nellie. I knew 'e'd try it on one day. He's not having them, no, he's not, never. He's crafty, he only wants them so when they're old enough he can send them out to work and get money from them. He's a wicked bugger, no mistaking.'

Nellie Garden wrapped her plump arms around the slim young woman. 'Nay, luv, don't fret, that slob won't ever get your girls cus I know as you'd never let him.' Hugging Lily to her, she continued, 'Let me mek you a cup o' char, you'll soon feel better.' Turning to head into the tiny kitchen, she saw the front doorway was crammed with women, all listening intently to what was going on. 'Come on now, you lot, stop being so nosy. The show's over.' Flapping a plump arm she promptly slammed and locked the door.

Suddenly, the letter flap rattled open and Babs called, 'Mom, let us in, please.' Her voice travelled through the flap into the dark living room, alerting Lily to the fact her daughters were locked outside.

'Thought you'd gone to the shop,' she cried, flinging the door wide.

'Ya d'ain't give us any money, Mom.'

'Ya could have had it on the slate, for Gawd's sake,' Lily remonstrated. 'Here y'are and I want the change as well.' She shoved a few coins into the outstretched paw. Hesitating for a moment, she carried on, 'Remember what I'm always telling ya, no speaking to strangers, right? And keep away

The Other Place

from that Freddy down the terrace who's got that there impetigo, I don't want ya catching that.'

Nodding, both girls tripped lightly down the garden path, through the rickety gate, and turning right, they walked towards Mrs Chance's corner shop.

'That was awful, our Babs,' Chrissie murmured. 'I was so scared that 'er with the big teeth would take us away from our mom. I don't wanna live with our real father. I hate him and always will for what he did.' Tears started trickling down her pale face.

Stopping in her tracks, Babs gave her sibling a quick hug, saying firmly, 'No one, just no one, will ever take us away from our mom. She wouldn't let them, silly. She loves us, and step-father does too.'

Actually, Babs had always sensed from the word go that their stepfather positively disliked them. The feeling was mutual; she detested Alf Brown and wished her mom had never married him. The older girl wasn't going to say this to her sister as she didn't want to worry her. Chrissie was younger than her and of a much more vulnerable nature. She rarely, if ever, stuck up for herself, preferring always to turn the other cheek when someone had a go at her.

***

'There's something about him I dislike intensely.' Babs confided her misgivings about her stepfather to her best friend, Sandra.

'What do you mean?' Sandra asked, cocking her

The Other Place

head to one side so that her long dark hair fell in a shiny sweep down below her shoulders. Sandra never worried about having nits; she got the tooth comb out every night without fail and spent hours combing through the silky strands. She always said she would never cut it, despite the daily threat of nits that rampaged throughout the school.

'Well, it's like this,' Babs replied, picking up a pretty flower-backed hairbrush and running it through her friend's hair. 'Sometimes I catch him watching us with a really resentful look on his fat face. He meks sure Mom's not in the room when he starts with his looks and nasty remarks, though; he's dead crafty is Alf Brown. He waits until she's getting the dinner on or mekkin' a cup of tea. Other times, when we're eating, I get the feeling he's watching our every mouthful and totting up the cost.' Then, passing the brush back to her friend, she continued, 'I hate his podgy little hands as well. When I see him shoving his food into his mouth, I shudder. I can't help it; he gives me the creeps, the slob.'

'Gawd, stop worrying, girl, you'll be getting married before you know it.' On these words Sandra let out a bellow of laughter, changing the subject smartly. 'Here, let's see if we have enough material to make our new skirts for the dance.' She was used to her friend's obsession with her stepfather's ways.

Sandra much preferred to talk about herself as she considered *she* was the most important person in her world. She was going places, and in fact she had told Babs on numerous occasions that she was going to be a famous film star. Really, she had no space inside her head except for herself. Sandra loved Sandra and she had plans.

In the main, Babs kept her feelings regarding her stepfather to herself. She knew her friend wasn't really interested in hearing her sounding off about Alf, but at times she couldn't help getting angry. It got it off her chest, and afterwards she could concentrate on Sandra's latest plans to achieve fame.

***

Babs was reluctant to mention Alf to Chrissie. She didn't want to upset her. What she didn't realise was that Chrissie also experienced the same feelings, but was unwilling to mention them to her for exactly the same reasons. Alf frequently took Chrissie aside and told her she was stupid and a daftie, and he would shout and threaten what he would do to her if she told anyone; he frightened her. She avoided him whenever she could. He revelled in dominating his youngest stepdaughter.

Bending down, Chrissie carefully tugged her ankle socks up as she didn't want to make the holes in them any bigger, but they kept disappearing into her black lace-up shoes. She gave a little wriggle and a tug at her waistband.

'What yer doing, Chris?' Babs asked, smirking.

'You know as well as I do,' she giggled. 'Me drawers keep slipping down. I wish our mom or you would tighten the elastic in them for me.'

'I'll do 'em tonight; come on, let's hurry or

The Other Place

Mom'll be after us.' As an afterthought, she asked, 'You okay now?'

Nodding, Chrissie averted her eyes. She was thinking, *No, I'm not really, but I can't tell you about the ghost of the soldier who was following the woman with the big teeth cus you didn't see him.* Holding hands, they made their way to the corner shop, each sister deep in their own private thoughts.

Chrissie was thinking about Amelia, who at one time had been her best friend. She could tell her anything and know for certain not a word would ever be repeated to Babs or any other family member. The trouble was she hadn't seen her for some time.

She had first met Amelia, or Amy for short, many years ago, after being shouted at and bullied by some lads in the school playground. As she walked home, a girl had suddenly popped up beside her, saying, 'Hello, my name's Amy, may I walk home with you?' Nodding glumly, Chrissie had agreed. Much to her delight, her day brightened after looking into the smiling sea-green eyes of her new friend. She thought how pretty she was and admired the way Amy's blonde hair curled in long ringlets beneath her dark blue bonnet.

But she couldn't understand why the girl was wearing a bonnet. Nobody wore a bonnet, except in picture books in the library; girls wore pixie hoods nowadays. Chrissie was puzzled by the girl's appearance as a whole. She wore a long blue dress, black button boots peeping out beneath her dress, and a dark blue short cape. Chrissie couldn't remember seeing this girl in her school, but

The Other Place

strangely enough she thought she recognised her. Casting a surreptitious glance at her new friend, she was greeted with a glowing smile, and linking arms they skipped happily along the dusty pavement, chattering away as if they had known each other forever.

Amy always seemed to be around when Chrissie needed her. Whenever the school kids teased her in the playground, calling her lanky and ugly, Amy always visited her later and cheered her up.

Sometimes Alf cornered her in the kitchen when Lily was out and would pinch her hard at the top of her arms, where it wouldn't show. Later on, as if by magic, Amy would sit beside her on the doorstep whispering words of comfort until she stopped crying.

A few of her fears had abated since her new friend had entered her life.

***

Giving her sister a squeeze, Babs followed her into Mrs Chance's shop and they quickly made their way to the magazine and comic shelf.

'Come on, girls, it's not pocket-money day.'

Mrs Chance's voice brought them down to earth fast; swiftly altering course they made their way to the counter where, much to their delight, the plump cuddly woman gave them each a stick of liquorice. One thing they both loved was to look at the shelves where the bright, shining jars of sweets stood. The best in their eyes was the jar of yellow kali. Chrissie's mouth watered at the thought of it.

The Other Place

She adored the wonderful fizzy taste as it exploded like shooting stars in her mouth. She couldn't wait until Saturday when she could treat herself. Babs' eyes took in the jars of barley sugar, bulls' eyes, gobstoppers, mints, and other mouth-watering sweets and chocolates that she liked. She wished they were rich so she could buy every favourite sweet and comic she wanted. *One day I will have everything I want,* she told herself, paying for the loaf of bread and heading home.

'Stop scuffing your pumps, our Chris, you know our mom will clip your ear if she catches ya doing it.'

Chrissie stopped immediately and together, arm in arm, the girls made their way home in the gathering twilight, chattering away like two sparrows about the sweets and comics they would buy on Saturday. The mention of Saturday reminded them of their favourite meal of the week: bubble and squeak with bacon, and the fat from the bacon poured over everything. How the sisters enjoyed that meal. Just thinking about it made their mouths water. Another favourite dinner was soused herrings. Bread and milk with sugar for breakfast was their all-time favourite, as were cocoa and sugar sandwiches for tea, or sometimes, if they were lucky, condensed milk sandwiches. Not that they were always that well off to enjoy these treats, but on the rare occasions when it was put before them, the food was greeted with cheers.

Later that night, cuddled up beside each other in the old double bed they shared, their mother's voice drifted upstairs; she was telling their stepfather about the day's events.

Babs choked back the lump in her throat hearing her mom crying about their real father wanting them back.

'How could he?' Lily demanded of Alf. 'He's never even clapped eyes on Chrissie, and he only saw my Babs a couple of times before he disappeared, going off with any woman who would have him. He even had a couple of kids by one woman, that's downright disgusting in my book.'

Hearing her mom's distress, Babs found she was having great difficulty in holding back her tears. *My poor, poor mom,* she thought, trying not to cry aloud as she didn't want to disturb her sister who was fast asleep beneath the old blankets and coats thrown over the top to keep them warm. Lily couldn't afford an eiderdown for them. She'd had it so hard when he upped and left her. *I can't imagine what she went through having no money coming in and us two to look after. Thank goodness our Gran helped look after us while Mom went to work. What a brave woman Mom is. She could quite easily have put us in a home.* Rubbing her eyes and drying her tears on the sheet, she heard Alf trying to comfort her mother.

'There's no way that scumbag would ever get custody of the girls. After all, I'm their legal guardian.'

Now, that's interesting, Babs speculated, *why didn't he adopt us? Why a legal guardian, I wonder what that means?* She fell into a deep sleep, her arm protectively wrapped around her sister.

Chrissie's crying out awakened her. 'There's something moving in the bottom of the bed. Mom,

The Other Place

Mom, come here.' She was screaming even louder. 'Come quickly, there's something in our bed.'

'Oh my God, Alf, wake up. Me girls are in trouble.' Lily fumbled to pick up a candle and a box of matches then quickly ran into their bedroom where she lit the candle. She threw back the bedclothes. The sisters huddled together by the bedroom door.

Alf shoved them out of the way just as Lily squealed, 'Oh no. The damn cat has had her kittens in the girls' bed.'

Both girls shrieked loudly in alarm and ran into their mother's bedroom; quickly pulling the grey army blankets back, they snuggled into the bottom of the bed.

'Yuk. I feel sick,' cried Chrissie.

Babs was more concerned as to the fate of the kittens. She knew her mother would drown them in a bucket of water. Lily had no choice, really. They couldn't afford to keep them. She shuddered, this time not with the cold but at the thought of those poor dear little kittens dying in such a manner.

Hearing Greg starting to cry, Babs leapt out of bed and picked him up from his mattress on the floor, as they couldn't afford a cot. She put him between her and Chrissie. There was no way they would sleep in their own bed that night.

Strangely, nothing more was said about the events of that day, but they became imprinted on the girls' minds for all time. Years later, they often discussed the woman with the horse's teeth and the horror of the cat having her kittens in their bed.

The Other Place

***

The girls liked to visit Birmingham City Centre, and before Lily married Alf it was a favourite Saturday treat for the three of them to walk up Gooch Street and into town together. They enjoyed wandering around the stalls in the Bull Ring market and listening to the traders shouting out their wares. The only things they disliked seeing were the rabbits, hares and birds hanging up in the butchers' stores. Seeing the dead creatures would bring a rush of tears to Chrissie's eyes, and Babs would feel sick. The smell of the dead birds would also make them hold their noses. The worst was the fish market, how they disliked that! The dead eyes of the fish seemed to glare out at them accusingly as if blaming them for being killed. Chrissie would shudder in fright and hide her eyes, pictures of the beautiful creatures swimming free in crystal seas would fill her mind's eye. She disliked this side of market life. If she could have avoided it, she would. At times her imagination would run riot after she had eaten meat or fish, imagining that the creatures were actually alive inside her. She would feel sick at the thought of it. A nasty taste would linger in her mouth for days.

Lily would laugh at them when they complained about the smell of the fish, saying, 'Huh, you should smell the sauce factory. I've smelt it some days when you ain't with me. I can tell you, that vinegary smell nearly knocks your head off.' The girls doubted it; they enjoyed HP Sauce if ever they were lucky enough to have it. Their mom would

The Other Place

water it down with vinegar or water to make it last longer. The same as she made the tea last and last by constantly refilling the teapot with hot water.

All the barrow boys admired Babs, her daintiness along with her striking blonde hair and blue eyes drew their attention, and they would give her an apple or an orange, "for looking beautiful". Lily would sniff, feeling sorry for her younger daughter, Chrissie, who rarely received a compliment. She did notice her youngest daughter never seemed to mind. Chrissie just accepted that her sister was the good-looking one and always would be. Truth to tell, she *didn't* mind – she preferred to remain in the background. Not that she was ugly, far from it; she had lovely thick, wavy, honey-blonde hair complemented by sea-green eyes. She was tall and well built, but Babs' startling beauty overshadowed her every time.

Ever since Lily had married Alf, the girls stayed at home on a Saturday, looking after Greg and cleaning the house while Lily went up town with her husband. Lily would occasionally buy them a small gift from Woolworths; sometimes it was a comic or sweets, just something to say she had thought about them while she was out. The girls treasured these gifts from their mom, but Babs often caught a gleam of resentment in Alf's eyes when Lily gave them the gifts, although it was gone in a flash when he caught her gaze. She couldn't wait for the day when she could leave home and Alf Brown behind.

The Other Place

CHAPTER 2

One Monday morning, Chrissie was sitting waiting on the doorstep while her sister helped Lily in the washhouse just across the yard. Monday had always been Lily's day for doing the weekly wash, and she shared the morning with a couple of other neighbours, so her mom was up bright and early to light the boiler and get cracking. Babs helped as much as she could before it was time for school. Chrissie had helped beat the rag rug and was patiently waiting to go to school. She smiled to herself remembering her many chats with Amy. In her heart of hearts she knew her friend was not real, but at times doubt would creep in when a small voice whispered inside her head that she was. It didn't really matter because Amy had helped her through her schooldays when the bullies had tormented her, and Amy had been there to support her when Alf bullied her. Chrissie adored Amy, she was the best friend a girl could have.

Hearing Babs calling her, Chrissie dashed inside, picked up the two small lunch packets of dripping sandwiches from the table, and ran as fast as she could to catch her sister's disappearing figure.

That evening Lily told them they were moving house.

'Moving?' the girls chorused. 'Where to, what about school and our friends?'

The Other Place

'The council has given us a new house in Fellfeld. It has an inside toilet.' Lily's eyes gleamed at the thought of this. 'No more potties to empty in the mornings, girls, and,' hands on hips, she continued happily, 'we'll have a front and back garden. Bigger rooms as well.' She almost whooped with delight. 'No more of this.' She waved her arm around indicating their lack of space. 'We'll have room to breathe.'

Babs suddenly noticed her mom's stomach was swollen. Another baby was on the way. Funny she hadn't noticed before, but her mom's pinafore had probably hidden it. She almost groaned aloud – more smelly nappies and sickly smelling baby clothes soaking in the old white chipped enamel bucket, and airing all day and night on the fireguard, steaming all the windows up.

'How many bedrooms will there be, Mom?'

'Three, petal, more room all round,' her mom chirruped happily. 'It'll get us away from these slums. You'll love it, I'm sure.'

The girls glanced at each other in surprise. Slums? With raised eyebrows they wondered what she meant. This was their home, they knew no other. What did she mean by slums?

'What about Gran and the rest of the family?'

'Questions, questions.' Lily was getting impatient. 'Away with you both. We're off come Friday, so you'd better help me with the packing.'

On reflection, Babs realised why they were moving house so quickly; it was because of the woman with the horse teeth. Mom didn't want her or their real father coming to the house again. Mom was scared and Babs decided to tell Chrissie later, when they were in bed, about the new brother or sister they were going to have.

***

The girls found it strange having so much more room in their new home. They liked it and quickly adjusted. They soon found that the more room you have, the more you need, and the extra space in their bedroom quickly filled up. They did miss their Brook Land friends at first, but Babs soon made new friends. Chrissie found the move to the new school difficult. She found socialising hard and always felt separate from her peers. Sometimes Lily wondered why her younger daughter didn't mix with the other kids.

She would tell Chrissie to go outside and play, but inevitably, when she looked out of the window, she would see her leaning against a garden hedge simply watching the other children playing. Her daughter was at her happiest reading a book on the doorstep or just day-dreaming.

***

Babs was getting ready to go out with Alan, her latest boyfriend. Brushing her hair, she grinned, remembering when she and Chrissie had first met the two girls who lived next door. She had been in the back garden with Chrissie; they had been taking turns wheeling young Gregory up and down the path in his pram to soothe him while their Mom was trying to get their new home organised.

The Other Place

Hearing a noise in next door's garden, they gazed across the small wooden palings. Chrissie's mouth dropped as far open as it possibly could and she rubbed her eyes, blinked, and looked again, amazement written all over her pretty little face.

Babs shouted, 'Hello, twins.'

Her sister turned to her. 'Is that what they're called, sis, is that their names, Twins?'

'You what, don't tell me you ain't ever heard of twins?' Babs smiled, wrinkling her nose in surprise that her sibling had never encountered twins before.

'We're Linda and Daphne,' the girls chorused, rocking backwards and forwards on their Blanco-whitened pumps. Again, in unison, 'We're twelve years old and go to the school just up the road. Will you be joining?'

Watching their smiling faces surrounded by short, dead-straight black hair, Babs noticed how thin they were and thought what a shame it was that they both had to wear the same clothes as each other. 'I bet it gets on their nerves,' she muttered under her breath.

'Dunno,' she shouted back, 'but we'll see you there on Monday if we do.' Chrissie was still dumbstruck and Babs nudged her, saying, 'Come on in, our Greg's asleep, we'll see if we can help Mom. We'll leave Greg under the kitchen window where we can watch him, make sure no cats get on his pram and suffocate him.'

***

The Other Place

Chrissie loved her new baby sister, Jessica, who was eighteen months old, and she would rush home from school eager to see what she had learnt that day. She adored telling her stories. Greg pretended he wasn't interested in listening to them – after all, the stories she told Jessica were a little childish for him – but he would sidle up and listen in. When she put Greg to bed he always asked her to tell him a story. Chrissie had no problems in making up new stories for her siblings.

She was happy in her new home, but missed Amy dreadfully. Chrissie had always been shy, but since moving house she had found social situations increasingly difficult.

Chrissie was distressed when she discovered she had passed the rising twelves' entrance examination granting her a place to attend the grammar school. Lily had said firmly that she had to attend the new school. Lily overruled every objection and Chrissie reluctantly accepted that she had to go.

She needed a friend to talk to at this time but Amy was no longer around. She missed their chats on the step. More so now as Babs was quite the grown-up young lady and had made lots of new friends, including boys. Despite her love of Jess and Greg, she yearned for a chat with her old friend.

Chrissie nearly jumped out of her young skin when she suddenly heard Amy's voice saying, 'Hello.' Turning her head she was delighted to see her. 'Where've you been?' she queried.

'Oh, just around,' her friend replied airily.

'I've missed you. I enjoy our chats.'

'I knew you'd be busy moving into a new

The Other Place

house, new grammar school, and a new baby; so many new beginnings to keep you occupied.'

'What brought you back?'

'I thought it was about time I came to say hello.'

'I'm glad you have.' Snuggling up beside her friend, the youngster chatted about her day and the homework she had to do after tea. She went on to describe her baby sister; in fact, she hardly drew breath in the next fifteen minutes, until a shout from the kitchen alerted her to her mother.

'I have to go in, Mom wants me –please come and see me again.'

'Oh, we will meet again, have no doubts about that.' With a mysterious smile, Amy disappeared.

Trotting happily into the kitchen, she realised how much better she felt for having had such a good chat with her old friend. Strange how Amy knew so much about her; Chrissie was pleased she had said they would meet again.

'Chris, come on, help me with the tea, our Jess wants a kiss and cuddle, you know. I hope you wiped your feet, I've just cleaned the floor. By the way, they've been mithering me to tell them a story. I ain't no good at that sort of thing, I told 'em you'll tell 'em a story later on. I know you enjoy making 'em up.' Her mom smiled cheerfully, stirring the rabbit stew that was bubbling merrily on the cooker. 'You can make the tea, but hold the kettle with a tea towel when you take it off the stove or you'll burn your hand, like you did the other day. You day-dream, Chrissie, that's your trouble.'

The Other Place

Lily was happy, having moved from the back-to-back house in Brook Land to this new home; knowing she had left her ex-husband behind was a huge relief. *He won't find us here,* she frequently told herself. *He did us a big favour sending that woman and threatening to take the girls away. At least by me telling the council, they soon got us moved to the top of the slum clearance list. That ratbag had no rights to send anyone to the house like that.* Just thinking about that day and other long-buried painful memories upset her, and she surreptitiously wiped a tear from her eye.

'What's up, Mom?' Babs asked anxiously, bursting through the back door and seeing her mother wipe her eye on the corner of her floral pinafore. 'Is one of the kids ill or is it Grandma?'

'No, lass, you worry too much, it's the onions and leeks in this 'ere stew I'm stirring that's mekking me eyes water, that's all.' She quickly slammed the memory door.

'Oh, I'm glad you're all right.' Hardly drawing breath, Babs went on, 'Is it okay if I go to Sandra's tonight? I haven't seen her in ages and ages.'

Lily hesitated for a second. 'Mmm, best ask your dad first, luv, the nights are beginning to draw in.'

'But he ain't my dad, is he?' As soon as the words were out of her mouth, Babs could have bitten her tongue off. 'Oh, I'm sorry, Mom, really I am, but why do you always have to ask him first? I'm only going to see Sandra, my best friend, for goodness sake, I'm not going off with a load of Teddy Boys, you know. This is the 20th century, and I go out to work. Girls do go out on their own,

The Other Place

you know. What's it to do with Alf anyway?' Her whole demeanour spoke of self-righteous anger and Lily bobbed her head in acceptance.

'All right, my girl, but I want you home by nine at the latest. Like me, Alf's worried about you being out on the streets after dark, you don't know who's about nowadays, those Teddy Boys go about in gangs looking for trouble, and we don't want you getting hurt.' Secretly, Lily was terrified her daughter would fall for a baby and didn't think she could stand the shame an illegitimate child would bring to her family. The thought of what Alf would say was unthinkable.

Babs sighed. 'I'm not a child, Mom, and you have to learn to trust me. The bus stop is only at the end of the road, you know – blimey, if you stand outside on the pavement you can see me getting on and off it.'

Five minutes later, Babs was off with a cheery, 'Bye all see yas later.' She was relieved to get out before Alf arrived home. It was good to avoid him and his snide remarks.

Chrissie watched her sister tip-tapping her way down the road in her white stiletto heels, her navy-blue spotted circular skirt flaring around her slim legs. Chrissie thought she looked beautiful; occasionally she caught glimpses of Bab's lovely pink-edged flouncy net underskirt. Chrissie hoped against hope she would own one in the future.

Strangely, Chrissie wasn't envious of Babs; she missed her company, but was glad she was happy in her work and her relationship, and she was certain her sister would eventually marry Alan.

The Other Place

'Now what do I do?' she asked herself. 'Mom and Alf won't want me sitting downstairs with them tonight.' Not that she ever felt welcome when Alf Brown was around. She never thought of Alf as her dad. He was just Alf and always would be.

She wandered gloomily down the narrow, uncarpeted staircase, which was always well-scrubbed by Lily, through the kitchen and sat on the doorstep. *I'll be fourteen this year, and if I hadn't passed for the grammar school I'd be leaving next year. Why did Lily make me go?*

Alf had railed against spending the money on her uniform and gym stuff. For once, his wife had stood up to him and insisted Chrissie was going to the grammar school. That was one argument Alf Brown had lost.

'I have to do an extra year and I really dislike that place,' she muttered, as she sat disconsolately, head in hands, trying to think of a way of getting out of attending the awful school. Suddenly, she felt dizzy and coloured lights flashed in front of her eyes.

She became aware she was somewhere she had never been before. It was misty and cold. She shivered. The sun was rising behind a cluster of trees. Despite the cold, she realised how beautiful her surroundings were. The sun's rays touched everywhere, the trees shimmered as the sun rose higher in the sky, and a light frost glistened across the grounds. Chrissie was enthralled by the place and tried hard to recognise it. Gazing around, she saw a dog in the distance; he was running about obviously enjoying himself. She was awestruck by

The Other Place

this beautiful place.

'What did you say, Chris?' her mother's voice shouted from the kitchen, breaking the magical scene.

'Nothing, Mom,' she called back, shaking her head and stretching, dispelling the giddy feeling. She dusted her gymslip off and, dragging her feet, she made her way to her bedroom, puzzled at what had just happened to her.

Lily listened to her daughter's slow progress up the stairs, worrying why she seemed so miserable lately. *You don't have to be a psychic to realise she's missing Babs*, she mused. Pulling the metal curlers from her hair, she scratched her head in relief, glad to be free of them. She did remember a time a few years ago when Chrissie had become quieter than ever. She blamed Alf for that and had honestly thought her daughter would forget what had happened. *She probably has*, she reassured herself. Remembering it also worried her, so she promptly closed her mind to what had happened; Lily Brown allowed no room for guilt in her life.

'They're vicious, them curlers. It'll be nice when the manufacturers invent something new,' she grumbled to herself, rubbing her tender scalp. Her head always felt sore when she took them out, yet she wore them every day, normally with a headscarf tied turban-wise around her head. Lily had a permanent headache. Making a cup of tea she mused on the fact that her second daughter was growing up, and that possibly accounted for her strange moods of late.

The Other Place

***

'I don't think Chrissie is interested in boys yet, though she's not far off,' she remarked to Alf later that night. His head was firmly buried in the *Evening Mail* sports page. He just grunted. Alf never wanted to discuss the older girls. He had no interest in them at all. He had never even changed the older girls' names from James to Brown.

Mmm, Lily thought, *if I'd mentioned little Jessica, he would have been chatting about her non-stop. The sun shines out of her backside, whatever she does.* Testing him, she asked, 'You know what our Jess did today, Alf?' The paper rustled as he quickly folded it in half, a huge smile splitting his chubby face, making his dark eyes look like tiny currants.

'Oh, what's that lovely babby done today? She's a clever one, no mistaking.'

Narrowing her blue eyes, Lily hissed, 'Ain't that just like you, Alfred Brown? Mention one of the other girls and you more or less ignore me, mention our Jessie and your lugs practically fall off the sides of your head. Sometimes you mek me sick and what's more, what about our poor little Gregory? He hardly gets a look from you, unless it's to tell him he's done summat wrong.

'Well,' she added on a huge intake of breath, 'let me tell you, it's about time you showed an interest in the rest of this family. It's obvious to one and all who you love the most, and no mistaking.'

Alf was astonished to say the least. His chubby cheeks flushed at his wife's strong words, and he spluttered, 'I dunno what's got into you, Lil. I work

The Other Place

hard for all of you, and well you know it.'

Lily nodded her head. 'But you ignores us all, Alf, and it ain't right. The other kids feel it, you know, when you're forever fussing over young Jessie.'

Alf sat pensively, ruminating on her words; he was startled. Lily had never said so much to him in one outburst since they had married. He loved his two kids, but if he was honest with himself, yes, Jess was his favourite, and he did resent the older girls. They got on his nerves, especially that daft Chrissie; mind you, Babs was an arrogant little sod as well. Personally, he'd be more than glad when they left home, but he hadn't better say that to Lily. Jess after all was their daughter, and was so pretty with her blonde bubbly curls and blue eyes; who could fail to love her?

'Excuse me, Lily, but Chrissie adores Jess, you know she does.'

'They all love Jess, Alf, but you never ever show the others any interest. That's all I'm saying. Babs and Chrissie will be gone before you know it.'

His eyes opened wide, wondering what she meant.

'I mean Babs will be married, if that Alan she's seeing asks her, she's crazy about him. Chrissie will be finishing school and going to university. We could be grandparents before we know it.'

'Blimey, Lil,' he blustered, going a bit pale at the suggestion of being a grandparent, 'at least give Chrissie a chance, 'er's still at school.' He growled as he lit a Capstan and rattled the newspaper.

Alf knew he would never acknowledge either of

The Other Place

the two older girls' children as his grandchildren, if they had any. No way; after all, they weren't of his blood. He would have been ecstatic if they'd gone back with the woman their father had sent to the old house. Nothing would have pleased him more. He and Lily would have been a family in their own right. As for Lily thinking that daft Chrissie would ever get into university, he wondered which planet she was on.

Lily knew their conversation was at an end and she thought, *Well, I tried, kids, we'll have to see if it makes a difference.*

***

Chrissie lay in bed remembering the misty place she had briefly been transported to where the sunlight was breaking through the trees. She felt she had visited it before. The whole episode confused her and she didn't know whether to tell Babs about it or not. Perhaps not, her sister might think she was making it up. She'd be glad when her sister came home.

Despite Bab's vehement protests, Chrissie insisted on sleeping with the window open. She hated being in any room without a window or door open. Crowds terrified her. Even thinking about being cooped up upset her and she would feel panicky.

If anyone stood too near her, the need to get away became immediate. How she wished she could be 'normal' and not have these awful feelings.

Because of this problem, Chrissie had become

The Other Place

withdrawn and antisocial, preferring to keep her own company than mix with the other kids in the street; she made no school friends. If only she could find a way to relieve the feeling of panic she would be overjoyed.

Lying as still as she possibly could, she remembered the beautiful frosty, misty morning she had seen and felt as if she was being drawn back into it. This time she noticed the leaves were a wonderful golden brown, but as the early morning sun sparkled on them, they changed to a burnished gold. She had to touch them. Bending down, she grasped a few. She could smell the damp soil and feel the sun-warmed leaves. A gorgeous light lit up the whole scene and Chrissie felt as if she was in a mysterious, magical place. A contentment she hadn't experienced for years stole over her, and she drifted into a dreamless sleep.

Creeping into the bedroom later that night, Babs saw her sister sleeping peacefully. Taking a closer look she was more than surprised to see a few leaves scattered over the quilt, and picking them up she wondered where they could have come from. Chrissie wouldn't have brought them in and put them on the bed. In fact, they felt a bit damp.

Moving quietly around the bedroom so as not to disturb her younger sister, she slipped off her stilettos, and casting a fond glance at the sleeping girl, she noticed another few leaves entangled in Chrissie's hair and gently removed them. She wondered again as to where they might have come from. Chewing her lip, she tried to work out why

The Other Place

her sister would bring leaves into the bed, but no solution presented itself. Carefully folding her clothes before placing them at the bottom of the bed, she slipped between the bedclothes, doing her best not to wake her sibling.

Babs soon forgot about the leaves as she recalled Alan's passionate kisses when they'd whispered good night. She blushed remembering how excited Alan had become. She was certain the snogging would go no further. Alan respected her. *Worse luck*, a voice whispered mockingly; she blushed even more and buried her head deeply into the pillow. Sleep dragged her down into a wonderful dream of marrying her beloved, and of the blissful carefree life they and their children would live together.

Chapter 3

All the following day at work, Babs looked forward to seeing Alan; just thinking about him made her heart skip a beat, and remembering how his kisses set her senses alight filled nearly every waking moment. Finding herself unable to concentrate on her work, she gave a mental shrug, realising that if she lost her job she would be in big trouble with Mom and the awful Alf.

Thoughts of home ran through her mind as she tidied the work files, and she recalled Alf's possessiveness towards Jess and worried how it would affect the youngster as she grew up. Her mother's face swam before her, and she wondered if Lily did really care about her and Chrissie. Lily hardly ever showed them any affection whereas she was always hugging the other two, Jess admittedly more than Greg. There again, Greg was all boy, and would push Lily away, saying 'Don't be daft, Mom, leave me alone.'

She reflected affectionately that Greg was growing into a nice lad; despite being a bit of a tearaway at times, he was a very intelligent boy, and she worried about the way Alf ignored him most of the time. She'd often seen the look of longing in Greg's young eyes when Alf was making such a fuss of Jess. *At least Mom tries to make it up to him,* she mused, flicking through her files; *let's hope it's enough and Greg doesn't grow up with a huge chip on his*

The Other Place

shoulder.

Chrissie sprang into her mind. She also worried about her young sister, as she hadn't been spending any time with her lately. Babs felt guilty about this but shrugged her shoulders, hoping her sister would understand that she had to work, help Mom and spend time with Alan. *Life can be so difficult at times,* she deliberated, glancing across at her colleagues in the open-plan office at the Co-op. *Chris will be fine,* she comforted herself; *after all, she'll be starting work next year.* She thought it was a pity Chrissie didn't want to go to university; strange how she never really made any friends, just acquaintances, always reading and scribbling her stories in her bedroom, and sitting day-dreaming on the doorstep; that about summed her sister up, in *her* eyes.

She worried why her sibling had developed the habit of having to sleep with the bedroom window or door open. She didn't know what could cause this. Poor Chrissie, at times she seemed to be a very disturbed youngster.

Finding Alan springing to the forefront of her mind again, she told herself to forget about everyone and get on with her work or she would be in big trouble.

***

After an early evening snack of sandwiches and French cream sandwich cake at Lyons Cafe in New Street, Babs and Alan made their way up to the Gaumont cinema. They walked past the flower

The Other Place

sellers who were packing up to go home, the hot-potato man shouting his wares at the top of his voice, the newspaper vendors trying to outdo each other selling the *Evening Mail*, and the handy-carrier man on the verge of putting his goods away for the day.

To Babs, the sounds and smells of the city were wonderful, she revelled in all of it; along with the traffic noise, it spelled home to her. She adored the city and when she was there with Alan her happiness was complete. She loved both with a passion. The busy streets and crowds of people in town made her feel part of the world, and she wished she had Chrissie's way with words to describe just how she felt. She felt as if the city was part of her makeup, and wished that she and Alan could live in a flat in the city centre when they married, but common sense told her that this would never happen, as they would never be able to afford it. She wished he would propose to her, how she longed to hear the words, '*Marry me, Babs*'. She was certain it was the thought of what his mother would say to him that stopped him proposing. She was well aware his mother disliked her.

The perfect day out for Babs would be to walk around the shops with Alan all day long, to feel a part of the city's beating heart was all she asked. Days in the country or at the seaside were not for her; a day out in Birmingham with Alan was all she ever asked. Sitting in Lyons Cafe, people-watching, she was as happy as she would ever be. Babs never wanted to move away from Birmingham.

The Other Place

***

Babs suddenly felt she had to contact her mother immediately. 'I'm going to ring the phone box on the green,' she told a shocked Alan. 'Anyone who's passing it will fetch Mom for me. I've done it many times before.' With these words she quickly ran into a nearby call box and was soon connected to Lily, who shouted down the phone to her.

'Oh, Babs, thank goodness you've phoned; I was praying that ya would.'

'Mom, what's wrong?'

'It's our Chrissie. I can't find her,' her mother's tinny tones echoed down the line.

'What do you mean, you can't find her?' Clutching Alan's arm tightly she tried to absorb what Lily was saying. It was quite a tight squeeze in the phone box with Alan, but she found his presence comforting.

'The last time I saw her was a few hours ago – can you hear me, our Babs?'

Hearing the anxiety in her mom's voice, she urged her, 'Yes, Mom, carry on. Where was she?'

'Sitting on the kitchen doorstep, you know that's her favourite place. It's a wonder 'er ain't got blisters on her backside.'

Babs blushed hoping Alan hadn't heard that remark. 'So what happened?' She was getting impatient; hearing the pips, she quickly put more money into the coin-box. 'Shall I come home?'

'Yes, please do, pet. I'm so worried I can't think

The Other Place

where our Chrissie is, she's never gone missing before – come straight home, luv, I'll skin her alive when she shows up.'

***

Lily was extremely worried. She had expected her daughter to be sitting on the kitchen doorstep when she'd finished chatting with Mary and Joan, her neighbours. She'd tripped her way happily back to the house. Going through into the kitchen, she was fully expecting to see her still day-dreaming on the back step. Not seeing her, she assumed she was in her bedroom and decided not to disturb her, thinking she was probably doing her homework. Lily checked Jessie was all right and got on with preparing the evening meal.

It was only later after cooking the meal and dealing with the others that she realised she hadn't seen or heard her middle daughter since returning from her chat.

She called up the stairs, 'Chrissie, your food's on the table.' No reply, which was strange, she thought, calling again; still no reply. 'She must be asleep,' she remarked to the others.

'Leave her be, if the girl's too lazy to come and help you, let her go hungry,' Alf spluttered miserably through a mouthful of Lily's cheese-and-ham pie. 'Her don't deserve anything.'

'Don't say that, Alf,' Lily replied protectively. 'Chrissie is a big help to me, she must be feeling poorly.' On this thought she practically flew up the stairs, nearly tripping on a loose floorboard in her

The Other Place

haste. Knocking on the girls' bedroom door, she called, 'Chris, you all right, luv?' Greeted by a deathly silence, Lily tapped again and poked her head around the door; gazing around she was astonished to see the room empty. Rushing inside, she anxiously looked around, not understanding where her daughter could be; taking a deep breath and thinking how daft it was, she knelt down and looked under the bed.

After checking the other rooms just in case her offspring was in one of them, she made her worried way back down the stairs.

Settling herself at the table, she looked at the other family members, asking if they had seen Chrissie at all in the last hour. 'If her ain't on the doorstep, her's up in her bedroom scribbling daft things in those exercise books. I bet you she's hiding away somewhere so as she don't have to do any jobs,' growled Alf, taking a huge spoonful of treacle pudding and custard. He gave a loud burp and continued shovelling the pudding into his mouth.

'How can you say that about her, Alf? I already told you she's a good girl and has always been a big help to me.' Lily was angry with him and could hardly eat her meal. She knew her daughter wouldn't go off without telling her where she was going; in fact, it was unusual for her to go anywhere apart from the shops, down the brook or very occasionally visit her gran, although that was a rare event. 'The thing is,' Lily remarked, 'Chrissie never goes far. She has no friends, never has had any, so where is she?'

The Other Place

Her husband appeared quite unconcerned as he tickled Jess under her chin, making her giggle. 'Quit worrying will you, woman, she'll turn up soon enough – as you say, she hardly ever goes anywhere, she's too daft to do anything on her own. You know she is, so what the dickens are you getting so agitated about?' He continued in a much louder voice, 'I don't want to hear another word about her, do you understand?'

Lily was astonished at his callousness. Rattling the plates in a rage as she cleared the table, she turned on him. 'How can you take that attitude when our daughter is missing, you unfeeling brute?'

'OUR daughter?' he sneered, 'this is OUR daughter, this precious little girl.' Picking Jess up, he cradled the toddler in his arms, gently kissing the top of her head.

'So the truth is out,' Lily shrieked in disgust. 'I've always known you've never given tuppence about my girls; well, I'm glad you've admitted it at last.' With these words she marched into the kitchen slamming the crockery into the sink. She attacked the washing up in a frenzy, muttering to herself the whole time about her unfeeling husband; calling Chrissie daft, how could he say that?

'Now then, Lil, I didn't mean it, but you must admit she is inclined to say some daft things.' Alf patted her shoulder, regretting his earlier words.

'Too late,' she snapped. 'I'll never forgive you for what you've just said – go away, leave me alone, saying my Chrissie is daft. That's unforgivable,' she shrieked. ''Er's just a kid and kids do say daft things

The Other Place

from time to time.'

'See, even you agree with me!' he sneered.

'You make me sick, Alf Brown – go on, buzz off. I've had enough of you.'

Alf backed away; he'd never seen Lily so angry and upset before. Shaking his head, he muttered, 'I don't understand women.' He decided he'd go across the road and chat to his mate Joe for a while until Lily calmed down. *I hope that bloody dreamy kid hurries up and comes home,* he reflected. *This is all her fault, going off and leaving my little Jess alone in the house, good job for her she didn't wake up, or she'd be in real trouble.* Thinking this made Alf's temper rise, and he walked back into the kitchen shouting to Lily.

'This is all that daft bloody Chrissie's fault. Think what'd have happened if the babby had woken up.'

'Well, she didn't wek up, did she, so just shut up and go away before I throw summat at you.' Lily was almost dancing with rage. Grabbing the poker from the hearth, she waved it threateningly at him.

By now, Jess was crying and poor Greg was holding her tightly; both were snuggled into the corner of one of the fireside chairs. 'Look how you've upset these two little uns,' Alf said, backing away and heading for the front door.

'Me?' Lily yelled, grabbing Jess in a hug. 'My, I've learnt a lot about your character today, Alf Brown, and no mistake. I d'ain't realise what an 'orrible sod you are.'

Her last remark was greeted by Alf yelling, 'That Chrissie is barmy. I remember her talking about her invisible friend years ago, how stupid is

The Other Place

that? Well, I put a stop to that stupid talk, didn't I? Now all she does is scream in the middle of the night, waking everyone up. She needs her head examining and no mistake.' The slamming of the front door followed his words. Lily watched her husband almost running across the road to his friend's house, clutching his paper.

'Typical bloody man,' she yelled, 'always on the bloody defensive when he knows he's in the wrong.'

Guilt suddenly smote her as she recalled what Alf had done to her middle daughter some years ago; she had always felt guilty about the incident. Not wanting to make Alf even angrier, to her shame she had done nothing to help her. Shrugging her slight shoulders, she called, 'Greg, come and get your jacket on, pet. We'd better go and see if we can find our Chrissie.' She buttoned his navy blue jacket up and grabbed hold of Jess, hoping Greg's legs wouldn't be too cold in his short trousers.

'Hold still, Jess,' she cried, fastening the reins on her in the pram, and with Greg hanging off the pram handle she trundled off towards the local brook. Heading down the road of semi-detached houses, tears pricked at the back of her eyes, and she swallowed hard, wondering what had happened to her daughter, regretting all the times she'd nagged and pushed her away. 'I should have listened to all her funny talk,' she sniffed. 'Poor kid was only having bad dreams an' I was always too busy to pay 'er any attention. I'll mek it up to 'er when 'er's back home,' she promised herself. Memories resurfaced again of what Alf had done to

The Other Place

Chrissie years ago – perhaps that had made her run away?

Seeing Babs hurrying up the road with Alan, she yelled out, 'Thank goodness you're here.' Wiping her eyes on the back of her thin hand, she added, 'Come with us, will you? I'm going down the road to the fields and to look along the brook. I know our Chris likes going down there sometimes to watch the water and things. Thank goodness it ain't foggy tonight. We've more than our fair share of that fog with all the coal fires and factories belching the smoke out. It stinks as bad as Saltley Gas Works.'

'You're right about the fog, Mom,' Babs replied. 'Where's Alf?' She regretted the words immediately seeing the look of anguish cross her mother's face.

'Him? He's a bit busy just now,' she responded evasively. 'We'd better hurry, it'll be dark soon and then what'll we do?' She gulped back a sob as she hurried along, pushing the heavy pram. Greg, picking up on his mother's unhappiness, started to cry.

'Don't cry, Greg, my luv,' Babs cooed, 'we'll soon find her. Here, come and talk to Alan.' Grabbing her brother she pushed him towards Alan, who had been feeling a little left out of the family conversation.

'Shall I push the pram for you, Mom?'

Shaking her turbaned head, Lily gripped the pram handle tightly. 'I'm okay, duck. I'm used to it. I ain't got any shopping in it.'

'All right, old chap?' Ruffling Greg's hair, Alan tried hard to be friendly with the youngster. Truth

The Other Place

to tell he hadn't a clue how to act around children, as he was an only child and his parents had rarely let him out of the house to mix with other children who lived in the street. "Never know what he might bring home from them dirty lot", was one of his mother's favourite remarks.

"True, Doll", was her husband's normal reply. He rarely went against her, preferring a peaceful life.

Alan worked as a bank clerk, something his mom would proudly tell one and all in the shops she visited daily.

"Our Alan's got a job for life". She never stopped talking about her son to anyone who would listen, which wasn't many as he was always her sole topic of conversation. Dolly Gray never talked to anyone about his relationship with Babs; she didn't think Babs was anywhere near good enough for her son and heir.

Alan had always had visions of himself shooting the rapids when he grew up, or being a big-game hunter. His mother soon put paid to those boyhood dreams and now he was ensconced in the bank seemingly for life. He knew his mother would be heartbroken if he told her just how much he hated his daily routine. One thing was certain, he vowed once he was married to Babs he would change his job as quickly as possible. Even if it meant bringing home a lower wage, he was certain that with Babs' income they would manage fine. Alan Gray had his and Bab's life mapped out to a tee and children certainly weren't part of the plan. But how could he get his mother to accept her?

The Other Place

***

'I'm okay, just worried about our Chrissie,' Greg muttered glumly, scuffing his grubby pumps along the pavement.

Peering over the hawthorn hedges and calling Chrissie's name brought no joy. They asked some of the gangs of youngsters who were hanging round the lampposts if they'd seen her. They all shook their heads but said they would keep their eyes open.

Jessie started to cry. Lily tried consoling her as she pushed the pram along the lane.

'Er's getting hungry, that's the trouble. We'd better go home, it's getting dark.'

'I'll go to the police station,' Alan offered. 'It's dangerous for her to be out in the dark.' He bit his lip nervously when he realised what he'd said. No way did he want to make matters worse.

'Okay, luv, thanks, perhaps it might be quicker if you phone them, when we get home.' Lily sniffed, having a hard job holding her tears back. She didn't want to break down in front of them all, but it was so hard not to. Her imagination had taken flight, wondering what had happened to poor Chrissie.

Remembering Alf's attitude, her tears dried fast as a spurt of anger flashed through her chest. 'That miserable toad,' she muttered, 'how could he leave me to go and search for Chrissie on my own? Thank God our Babs came home.' She gave her eldest daughter a tremulous smile. 'Thanks for coming home, me duck, and supporting me, you must be psychic phoning me like you did.'

Babs gave her mom a cuddle and helped her push the pram up Beggar's Hill past The Ash pub; she decided to hurry as she could see Lily was nearly at the end of her tether.

'She'll be back soon, Mom, don't you worry.' Babs knew the instant she uttered the words that her sister would, in fact, be home when they returned.

She was right; as they turned into the back garden, there was Chrissie sitting huddled up on the doorstep.

'Where you bin?' Lily yelled at her errant daughter. 'Where did you get all those dirty marks on your dress from?' Leaving the pram, she ran and started shaking her daughter, not in anger but relief. Despite her harsh words, Lily was relieved beyond measure that Chrissie was safely home.

'Well, come on, miss. Where've you bin?'

'Nowhere, Mom.'

'I'm not stupid, Chris, now just tell me. *Where have you been?*' she demanded, beginning to sound really angry.

'I can't remember, Mom, honest. It's like there's a big empty space in my mind. I can't remember, honestly.' Chrissie began shaking uncontrollably as huge tears slipped down her pale cheeks. 'Mom, that's the truth.'

Babs sat beside her, hugging her closely. Lily, Alan and Greg grouped around the girls, not understanding what had happened.

Seeing streaks of dirt covering her daughter's

dress frightened Lily. 'Tell me, Chris,' she said, louder than she meant to. 'For the last time, what's happened to you? Where has all this dirt come from?'

'I don't know, Mom, honest. I don't remember.' Sobbing harder, she moved even closer to Babs.

'Hang on, sis, you'll have me off the step. Mom, open the door, will you?' she was concerned about Chrissie and repeated it, 'Open the door, please, Mom, we'll all catch our death of cold out here.'

'Okay, Babs, keep your flipping hair on.' Slipping the key into the lock, she led the way into the kitchen. Alan pulled the heavy coach-built pram up the back step and pulled it backwards through the kitchen, as there wasn't enough room to turn it around in the small space, then into the front room. He marvelled how someone as tiny as Lily could manage to manoeuvre the heavy pram up and down the step.

Babs moved the fireguard back from the dying fire and held a double sheet of newspaper in front of it to make it draw up. Suddenly there was a whoosh as the paper caught fire, and she dropped it quickly into the fire. Using the tongs from the well-polished companion set on the hearth she dropped a few small lumps of coal on, and she was pleased to see them catch. After adding a couple of larger lumps, she gave the hearth a quick brush over and hooked the fireguard back around the fire. Lily had taught them well to keep the house safe from fire.

Bustling around the kitchen warming some milk for Jess's night-time bottle, Lily brushed tears of relief from her eyes; she was so happy that Chrissie

The Other Place

was safely home. Babs lit the gas under the vegetable stew to heat it up and began slicing bread. She wondered if anyone would have any appetite to eat.

'Poor Mom and poor little Chris,' she whispered, 'somehow I have a funny feeling that there's worse to come.'

'Where's Dad?' Greg asked no one in particular, gazing around expectantly.

Lily looked askance. 'He only went across the road to see his mate an hour or more ago. You're right, Gregory. Where the devil is he? What a flipping awful day this has turned out to be. There seems to be no end to it.'

Greg was more concerned now; he knew his mom only used his full name when she was worried about something.

When they were seated around the table eating the stew, Lily began to worry aloud where Alf could have got to.

'Perhaps he's gone to the pub with his mate for a pint,' Alan offered, wishing he could wipe his plate with his slice of bread. The stew was extremely tasty and he could easily enjoy another serving.

Thanking Lily for the meal, he offered to clear the table and help with the washing up.

'That's woman's work, son, but perhaps you wouldn't mind giving Jess the rest of her bottle?' Despite herself, she had to chuckle. 'Mind you, giving the babby a bottle is woman's work as well!' Jess still had the one bottle before going to bed. It helped settle her down.

The Other Place

Gingerly, Alan took the little girl in his arms wondering what to do.

Babs laughed and gave him instructions on how to feed a baby. He felt very uncomfortable holding the child and was worried in case she was sick on him or worse. He felt out of his depth with this tiny human being on his lap.

Leaving him holding Jess, Babs took the opportunity to run across the road to see where Alf was. She returned quickly.

'Erm, Mom, Alf left his mate's house ages ago.'

'Yer what?' Lily screeched, dropping a plate on the floor. 'Where the hell is he, then? Come on, tell me, Babs. What did they say?'

'They didn't know, Mom,' she said, scrambling across the brown lino to pick up the pieces of broken plate before the little ones cut themselves. Babs was worried. It wasn't like Alf to go off without a word. Her mom had suffered enough in the past without Alf starting to cause her anxiety.

'It'll be all right, Mom – come on, I'll make you a cup of tea and we'll see what we can work out.'

Moving the clothes horse with the damp washing to one side, she made her mother sit in one of the fireside chairs. Leaning over the fireguard, she threw a few lumps of coal onto the fire, jumping back as a spray of sparks hissed and spat from the coals. Casting Lily an anxious look, she reassured her. 'Mom, it will be fine, honest.'

Taking Jess from Alan, Babs glanced with concern at Lily who was as white as a sheet and seemed to have retreated into herself.

Deciding Lily would be better doing something

The Other Place

she handed the baby to her.

It seemed to work; Lily wrapped her arms around Jess's warm body. 'He'll be back, Babs. He wouldn't leave her. She's the apple of his eye.'

Nodding, Babs agreed. 'You're right, Ma, look at our Chris disappearing and then Alf.' She was relieved that Lily had stopped correcting her use of his Christian name. 'It's given you a shock. Think on, though, our Chris came back, and I expect Alf will in his own good time.' *I really hope he doesn't*, she thought bitterly. If anyone hated Alf Brown, it was Babs.

'You're a good girl, our Babs.' Lily reached out a careworn hand and patted her cheek. 'He's likely up the pub and will be home later. I mean, if he does go, we'll be having bread and margarine to eat with a bit of sugar sprinkled on it, cus we'll have no money for food. Oh, I won't put the horse before the cart. He'll be back. Come on, we have to get these kids to bed. Our Chrissie's quiet, ain't she? I hope she's all right.'

'I'll check on her and put Jess to bed. You sit and have a rest, Mom, you look done in.'

Collecting her sister's nightclothes from the fireguard where they had been airing, she gave Jess a quick top and tail then took her upstairs. After settling her down, she poked her head into their bedroom.

'You okay, Chris?' she whispered to her sister who was sitting in a chair by the open bedroom window. 'Want to tell me about it?' Shaking her head, Chrissie continued gazing out at the familiar street scene; she was finding it hard to understand

The Other Place

what had happened and just wanted to be on her own.

'Come on, sis, you can talk to me, you know; we've always shared our secrets.'

'Not all.'

'Mmm, true, but you know what I mean. If it makes you feel better, you can tell me anything.'

'The only thing I feel bad about is worrying our mom, but I didn't know what was going to happen, did I?' She gave a huge gulp, realising she'd nearly given too much away.

Deciding not to ask her anymore, Babs gave her a big hug. 'I'm glad you're okay, sis. I'd better see Alan off. He'll want to make his way home. You know where I am if you want to talk.'

'Do you think Alf is up the pub?'

Surprised at the use of her stepfather's Christian name, Babs shot a surprised look at her. 'I haven't a clue, but he'd better watch his step; Mom's not in the mood for any of his antics.'

Downstairs, Lily had her hands full, instead of having a rest she'd set to cleaning.

Babs saw Alan glancing at the alarm clock on the shelf and fetched his coat, apologising for the upset.

'Don't fuss, I'm just pleased the lass is home,' he responded, giving her a quick peck on the cheek, and left hurriedly.

She jumped on hearing her mother's voice crying out. 'He's gone, the bugger's gone and left me!'

Making her way swiftly upstairs, she nearly bumped into Chrissie and Greg who were rushing

The Other Place

into their parents' room.

'What do you mean, Mom? Where's he gone?'

'Look.' Lily pointed to the open drawers in a small cupboard. They were empty of Alf's clothes. She swivelled around, pointing at empty hangers on the pole that held their few clothes behind a curtain in the corner of the room. 'See, he's taken his new pair of trousers and just left his old raggedy ones. Babs, he's left us. I can't believe it. Why did he bugger off? We were only gone an hour or so.'

Lily sat on the bed, head in hands, crying, wondering what had gone wrong that day. 'Babs, what's happening to us?' she asked, taking a piece of rag from her pinafore pocket, wiping her eyes and blowing her nose hard. 'This morning we were just an ordinary everyday family. What made him leave? I can't think of anything that would make him leave our Jessica.'

Not knowing what to say, for once her eldest daughter was dumbstruck, amazed that Alf could up and leave her mother. She'd had a suspicion that something else was going to happen that day, and that Alf was involved, but not that he was going to leave.

Sitting beside her mother she put her arm around her slim waist, gazing around the bedroom with its fading flower-patterned wallpaper and a few cheap mats scattered around the floorboards. Well, it certainly wasn't posh, that was a fact, but it was a million times better than Brook Land. At least Jess had a cot to sleep in and there was even a lampshade, albeit old, covering the light bulb. That certainly was a step up the ladder.

'I'll help you, Mom, all I can, you know I will. I'm sure he'll be back.'

'He can stay away. I don't want him now. He's just like any other man. He's probably been stringing a young woman along, more than likely. Obviously I'm too old and past it for him,' Lily retorted angrily.

Knowing her hurt was making her mother speak in this manner, Babs gave her a squeeze.

'Come on, we'll put Gregory to bed, we don't want to disturb Jessica.'

***

Gathering herself together, Lily went slowly downstairs, worrying and wondering where her husband was.

'I know we argued a lot, but so do millions of other married couples, and I did tell him to go away,' Lily remarked anxiously, picking up one of Greg's jerseys that desperately needed darning.

Glancing across the room at her eldest daughter, who was busy back-combing her hair into a different style, she asked, 'Do you think it were my fault that he left us, our Babs?'

Stepping back from the mirror that hung above the old, highly-polished sideboard admiring her handiwork, she turned to look at her mother.

'No, I don't, Mom, even if you had the biggest row in the world, he didn't have to leave home like that. If he wanted out, he should have had the decency to tell you.' She sniffed angrily, biting her tongue as there was a lot more she would have

The Other Place

liked to have said. Not wanting to hurt her mother, she thought it best not to speak her mind.

With a final admiring glance at her new hairstyle, she made her way to the fireplace, and sitting in Alf's vacant chair, she watched her mother darning.

'I'll go to his mother's tomorrow, see if he's staying there,' Lily stated.

'Why not go to his works first, they're the nearest. Or better still phone to see if you can talk to him?' Throwing some small lumps of coal on the fire, Babs jumped up and went into the kitchen to wash her hands. 'Wanna cuppa, Ma?'

'That's a good idea.' Quickly changing tack, Lily asked, 'Where do you think our Chrissie went?'

'Haven't a clue where she could have been, Mom.'

'I don't know how I'm going to get that dirt out of her frock.'

'Soak it in some Rinso first,' she suggested. 'Oh, I'll do it now.'

Putting some washing powder into a bucket of warm water, Babs swished it around to dissolve and then dropped the dress into it. She hoped the detergent would remove the stains. As she squeezed the dress, pictures came into her mind of a young girl in a great deal of emotional distress; she couldn't see the girl properly because she was just out of her view. She hoped and prayed the young girl wasn't Chrissie.

'Oh no,' she whispered, frantically pushing the dress deeper into the bucket of soap suds, in a way trying to bury the image of the youngster's distress.

The Other Place

Telling herself she was imagining things, she carried the bucket to the kitchen sink.

'Is it coming out, Babs? We can't afford any more clothes, not even second-hand from the Rag Market, now Alf's gone.'

'Yes, this Rinso is good, Mom.' She shuddered seeing the black dirt staining the water. 'I'll leave it in to soak overnight. Stop worrying, Mom, we'll manage.'

'Best away to your bed, luv,' her mother's tired voice drifted into the kitchen.

Planting a kiss on Lily's pale cheek, for once she could think of no more comforting words. 'See you in the morning, Mom.'

***

Later, lying in bed, Babs thought back over the day's events – she was still in shock at Alf's and Chrissie's disappearance. She hoped against hope her sister would tell her what had happened.

Babs could not make sense of it, and despite her hatred of Alf, she could not believe that he would physically hurt or abuse his stepdaughter. *If he has I'll find him one day and he'll regret for evermore what he did to her,* she vowed angrily.

Beside her, Chrissie lay awake; she was trying hard to forget what had happened to her. She knew it was the only way she would be able to cope. She wanted to scream and run, to try and escape what had taken place. She felt breathless, frightened, full of anxiety, and her heart raced alarmingly. No one would believe her if she told them, she had to

The Other Place

forget it, pretend it had never happened. She started counting hoping this would make the terrible memories disappear; she sought oblivion more than anything.

***

Rushing downstairs the next morning, Babs was surprised to see Lily already had a line full of brilliantly white nappies blowing on the line. She also saw that despite everything that had happened, Lily had her hair full of curlers.

'Gosh, you must have been up early, Mom,' she remarked, hungrily snatching a slice of toast.

'Couldn't sleep,' came Lily's doleful reply. 'I'm going to ring his works then go up the Welfare to get some orange juice, cod liver oil and a jar of malt for Jessica. We're running low. I've got the coupons ready in me bag.'

Remembering the taste of the cod liver oil made Babs pull a face, but on the other hand, she had loved the orange juice and the malt.

'It's quite a walk for you, Mom, up Staff Road, will you go into the village first and then on to the Welfare?'

'Dunno, luv, depends what they say at Alf's workplace. If he ain't in work I wun't go up the village, we'll have to manage with the bit of food we've got.'

Noticing how pale and red-eyed her mother was, Babs poured her a cup of tea and added an extra spoonful of sugar.

'Not too much sugar, Babs, remember, I just

said we've got to be careful.'

'You look as if you need a bit of extra sugar, Ma, one more spoonful ain't gonna overstep the mark, is it? Rationing finished years ago and we won't go short so stop worrying.

'I hope things go okay for you today, Mom. I'd better get myself to the bus stop or I'll be late. I'll be thinking of you, and you can phone me at work if you need me.'

The buses were always crowded this time of the morning and she needed to be on time. Her office manager frowned on latecomers, and she realised her job was even more important now as she would probably be the only wage earner.

It suddenly struck her when she was sitting on the bus that she hadn't once thought of Alan that morning – in fact, since she had closed the front door on him last night, he hadn't entered her head. Perhaps it was a good job he hadn't asked his parents' permission to marry her. She knew his mother disliked her. She actively ignored her on the rare occasions she had tea at their home. She also brought other girls into the conversation, pointing out how wealthy their parents were. Babs had quickly got the message that should Alan ask permission to marry her, it would be refused.

They couldn't marry now. After all, she couldn't possibly leave home; her money was needed to help support the family.

Chapter 4

Lily was astonished when the girl on the switchboard at Alf's works said he hadn't clocked in that morning.

'You sure?' she shouted loudly down the phone. Lily found it hard to grasp that the person on the other end of a telephone line could hear you if you spoke normally. 'You certain he ain't clocked in?'

'I'm certain, madam,' was the response. 'The charge hand was adamant, Mr Alfred Brown has not reported for work today.'

Slamming the phone down, she darted out of the telephone box and, grabbing the pram handle, pushed it towards Staff Road. 'Jessica, girl, I don't know where your father is, but we'll have to find him. He's the reason I look so red-eyed this morning, the selfish sod, wait until I get my hands on him.' She knew Jess didn't understand her, but she had to sound off at someone or she would have broken down in tears. Lily Brown, formerly Lily James, was worried out of her mind as to how she was going to manage without her husband.

***

Looking through the school railings at break time, Chrissie wondered where Amy was; she desperately wanted to speak to her and wondered if she would ever see her again. 'Of course you will,'

The Other Place

Amy's voice whispered in her ear. Glancing around, expecting to see her friend standing beside her, she was disappointed that there was no sign of her. All she could see and hear were the other girls huddled in groups talking quietly; they had been told in assembly that someone in a nearby house was very ill, and to show their respect the children were asked to be quiet when in the playground. A few of the younger girls were playing skipping games. How she envied their ability to mix and play together. She would love to go and join them, but felt far too shy to ask. She would often watch the kids playing in the street, but never had the courage to go out and join in the fun. She was too scared.

She felt lonely and unhappy most of the time. The nights were the worst, when the feelings of being trapped inside her mind made her want to scream and shout aloud with fear. It wasn't so bad when Babs was there, but sometimes she was late coming home and the fear inside her would rise up, threatening to engulf her like a huge incoming wall of water ready to submerge and drag her away. It was so frightening that an occasional small whimper would escape from her, and then she had to bite her lip hard, occasionally making it bleed, in case her mother or one of the others heard her.

What Chrissie was unaware of was that sometimes she woke Babs with her screams of fear. Her sister would stroke her hair and soothe her until she settled down. Her sibling didn't like to ask her what was making her cry out in distress, in case she made matters worse. Babs assumed her sister suffered from night terrors that many youngsters experienced, never guessing the magnitude of her sister's distress. She hoped she would outgrow whatever frightened her.

Chrissie heard the teacher calling them in a quiet voice for classes to recommence; she had decided not to use the bell today. Making her way slowly to the line of girls queuing to re-enter the school, Chrissie felt bowed down with depression. She was longing for leaving day; the thought of work was very appealing. She was hoping to join Babs at the Co-op office. *My wages will help Mom if Alf doesn't come home,* she thought, chewing her hair disconsolately. She worried about her mother and how she was going to pay the rent and all the bills. She realised it was going to be hard for them to manage. She reasoned that if only she could leave school now, her wages would help them out.

***

Leaving work the following night, Babs looked around hopefully for Alan. There was no sign of him, and she sighed, filled with concern as to where he could be. One of a crowd of girls who were following her shouted, 'Where is he is, Babs, had a lover's tiff, have ya?' She heard some of the girls tittering at the catty comment, but chose to ignore it. She could smell the odour of the chocolate wafting over from Cadbury's factory, and because she was so worried today, it made her feel nauseous. Making her way home, she went over and over the events of the previous evening, thinking she may have upset him in some way.

The Other Place

'It's so strange, Mom,' Babs remarked, hanging her coat on the nail on the back of the kitchen door. 'He did leave very quickly last night, but I thought it was because he wanted to catch the last bus. It's all so strange – our Chrissie disappearing, Alf going off somewhere, and there's no sign of Alan. I can't keep up with all this. Still, at least our Chris is home now. That's a blessing. She's very quiet, have you noticed, Mom? She won't tell me where she went, has she told you?'

'Blimey, our Babs, you don't half rattle on! You're right, though, it's puzzling me as well is all this disappearing lark. I mean, what's going on? I haven't a clue where Alf has got to. I went across to his mate's house and they told me the same as they told you, that he wasn't there long at all. They assumed he was coming back here. Which he did, but then he took off with his things. Why on earth would he leave us in the lurch? It beats me. As to where your Alan could be, I just dunno, Babs, and that's the truth; best if you catch the bus to his house when we've had our dinner. Just pull that window open a bit, it's steamy in here with the cooking and all the clothes airing in the front room. It must be like this in a laundry.'

Babs didn't really want any food. She wanted to go straight to Alan's house and find out what was going on. Perhaps he was ill. There again, if he was ill no one would let her know.

Peeling the potatoes, she was only half-listening to her mom; realising she was being selfish, she said, 'Sorry, Mom, I can't think straight at the minute.'

The Other Place

Throwing the last potato into the saucepan, she grabbed her coat from the back door, saying, 'I'm off to see what's wrong with Alan – sorry again, Mom, we'll talk later.'

Lily nodded ruefully. 'See you later, Babs, I'm sure he'll be okay, probably just fancied a day off.'

Chrissie heard Babs leave and made her way downstairs. She was glad Alf had disappeared. The atmosphere in the house felt a lot better without him. Secretly, she hoped he would stay away forever. There would be no more rows between him and Babs, or her mother for that matter. How lovely that would be.

Seeing her mother's unhappy face made her feel mean, she knew Lily loved Alf. In fact, at times she had the feeling her mother thought more of him and the two younger ones than her and Babs. She couldn't help feeling resentful when they took the two youngsters out, leaving them to clean the house and cook the dinner. Babs got really angry about it and Chrissie would step in and try to be the peacemaker, but underneath she also felt rejected and unhappy. She was certain Lily would be happier if she found someone new. She was positive the house would have a far healthier atmosphere without Alf's presence, but to her mind Lily was obsessed with Alf Brown. Hopefully, one day she would come to her senses.

Jess had everything, she mused – new clothes, new toys, anything Alf spotted that he thought Jessie would like, he would buy. There weren't many nights when he didn't arrive home with a gift for his 'little sweetheart'.

The Other Place

It was hard at times not to feel resentful, Chrissie thought as she scrubbed the kitchen floor on her hands and knees. *I'm like blinking Cinderella, only I'll never go to a perishing ball.* At times, wringing the floor cloth out, even being mild-mannered she would pretend it was Alf Brown's neck and give it an extra twist.

Babs had always resented being one of the 'skivvies' and did her best to get out of the housework and babysitting.

'No way,' she would refuse, when asked to do anything. 'I ain't Alf Brown's slave.' It was only after Lily threatened her that she would sulkily help out. When she left school, though, she refused point blank. 'I ain't a servant or a child-minder. I pays for me keep and that's it.' Off she would flounce upstairs to get ready to go out with Alan.

Chrissie would step in at once. She hated confrontation. 'Don't worry, Mom, I'll do it. You go and have a cuppa.'

Since Alf had left, Babs had decided she would help out more by peeling the potatoes and doing various small jobs, but only if they didn't interfere with her lifestyle. Babs was determined to marry at the earliest opportunity and lead her own life. The trouble was Alan still hadn't plucked up the courage to ask his parents.

'Can I help you, Mom?' she queried. Chrissie had begun to realise that by keeping herself as busy as possible, it helped to keep the *thing* (as she called it) at bay. Rather than sit upstairs writing her stories or looking out of her bedroom window, she spent more time helping her mom. The extra energy she

The Other Place

was expending on this helped her to sleep better. Should she find herself lying awake frightened, she would try and think of something nice. At times this was hard as some of her memories were coloured by the arrival of Alf Brown, but she would remember how her gran had hugged her as a little girl, and how pretty Babs had been as a child, and the happy times they'd had before Lily had remarried. These memories would sometimes carry her into a peaceful sleep. Other times were horrific, and she would lie awake praying for the awful feeling to leave her.

'See to the babby, will you, luv? I can get the dinner done much faster if you have her. It's only bubble and squeak, but it's enough for tonight.' Slicing the corned beef thinly, Lily threw it into the frying pan along with the potatoes and cabbage, mixing them together, her mind all over the place wondering where Alf was and why he had left them.

Picking Jessica up, Chrissie prayed she'd never have to see Alf or any of his relatives ever again. She had always disliked him and anyone connected with him. She wanted it always to be like this, no Alf watching their every move, giving out dirty looks to her and Babs; it was great not having to put up with his snide comments when Lily wasn't about. She knew they would all adjust in time, and home would be a happier place. No more sly pinches or punches from Alf Brown – wonderful!

'Wonder where Alan is?' she mused, looking across at Lily who was busy dishing the dinner up.

'I wonder where Alf is,' came Lily's swift

The Other Place

rejoinder.

'Babs will have to warm hers up on a saucepan of hot water when she comes back,' Lily grumbled, putting the plates on the table. 'It never tastes the same warmed up, but that's her own fault, not mine.'

'Call our Greg, will you, Chris, and wash your hands before having your dinner.'

Moving quickly around the small kitchen, Lily wondered how she was going to cope financially if she didn't hear from Alf soon. She had the family allowance for the three of them and although it was only eight shillings each, it helped. Bab's contribution was a huge relief, but that was it. She knew she would have to find work or they'd be out on the street. Chrissie would have to leave school and look after the youngsters; there was no other way she could manage. Her thin face creased tightly with worry. Tears glazed her eyes making her blink hard.

'Ma, you okay?' Chrissie asked, coming into the kitchen.

Nodding dolefully, Lily began feeding Jess some bubble and squeak, her mind awhirl. She had to pay the rent and feed and clothe the kids. Without Alf's money coming in, what was she going to do?

'Got to get a job,' she mumbled.

'Oh, Mom, that'll be hard for you, I'll help,' she offered eagerly, 'I'll leave school.'

Lily went to interrupt, but Chrissie seized her chance.

'I'll be here to help with the kids, cus you'll have to leave early in the morning. Think, Mom, I'll

The Other Place

be able to cook the dinner for you and clean the house.'

Lily was relieved that her daughter had offered to look after the youngsters. 'I'll stay at home tomorrow, Mom, and help you. We'll work something out.'

'It's your education though, luv. I really wanted you to go to the university along Bristol Road and have a good career.'

'Not for me, Mom.' Taking a sip of her tea, Chrissie could hardly restrain her joy. She'd be leaving that awful school and she prayed that Alf would never come back. Apart from the *thing* that haunted her nights, she felt happier than she had in years. Wiping that memory away, she concentrated on making plans for the future.

'I'll be fine, Mom. I can get Greg off to school and look after our Jessie. I never wanted to go to university. I'm not the studious kind, never have been.'

'Happen you're right, luvvy.'

***

Babs stormed in later that evening.

'Whatever's up with you?' Lily stared at her wild-eyed eldest daughter.

'He said he don't want kids.'

'You what?' Lily screeched. 'Alan don't want kids? That's why he's ignored ya? Well, blow me down with a feather. He ain't normal, he ain't. I always knew he was strange, ever since he was refused to do 'is National Service, I thought there

The Other Place

was summat not right about him.'

'Oh, come on, Mom, Alan was only turned down cus he's got flat feet, you know. It ain't as if he ain't right in his head.'

Lily shot her a look as if to say, "You'll learn." 'Well, he's got horrid yellow teeth as well,' she muttered under her breath.

'Just leave him be, Mom, please.'

Crestfallen, Babs paced backwards and forwards in the small living room.

'He told me straight: when he held our Jessie the other night, he realised, he doesn't like little-uns at all and never wants one. I've told him I'll have to think about what he's said, to see how *I* feel about not having any kids.'

'He's bloody unnatural, that Alan. He's a long tall streak of nothing, him,' Lily hissed. 'Let him go, Babs, you love kids, and you'll regret it if you marry him.' Wiping her hands down her flowery pinafore, she took a piece of rag from her pocket and blew her nose noisily.

Babs grinned slyly. 'There are ways, you know, Mom.'

'Don't think that, you barmy mare.' Lily was really irate. 'He'd up and leave you if you had a kid.'

Babs shook her head stubbornly. 'No, he wouldn't. He would love it when I had it.'

Furiously, Lily shouted, 'You're being stupid, Babs.'

Chrissie had been watching this exchange open-mouthed. Ever the peace-maker, she chimed in.

'Babs, I'm leaving school and I'm going to look after the kids while Mom gets a job.'

Her words stopped Babs dead in her tracks. 'What did you say?'

Repeating what she'd said, Chrissie was all smiles. 'Now I think we all need a nice hot cup of cocoa.'

Lily rattled the poker in the fire setting sparks flying up the chimney. 'You're the biggest idiot in this world, Babs James, if you think he'd stand by you if you had a babby.'

'Forget it, Mom, I told you I'm not seeing him for a week at least. You see, he'll miss me that much he'll agree to anything.'

Lily snorted, taking a cup of cocoa from Chrissie.

'I'll be looking for work soon; I know there's a chance of Alf coming back, but in case he doesn't, I'll have to become a wage earner again.'

Hearing Lily say Alf might come back, Chrissie crossed her fingers. *Please no,* she prayed, *make him stay away for ever.*

'You're sure it's a good idea for Chrissie to leave school, Mom? She's very young.'

'Needs must, Babs. I can earn far more than Chrissie could if she got a job.'

'I suppose you're right, seems a shame though.'

'Come on, bed, it's been a long day. Who knows, Alf might be back tomorrow,' Lily announced optimistically. She failed to see the dark looks her daughters exchanged.

***

'I've got a proper job, no more charring for

me!' Lily danced around the room like a young girl, Jess held tightly against her. Gregory watched, amazed. The girls were delighted to see their ma looking so happy. Twelve months had passed since Alf's disappearance and the family had struggled to make ends meet. Chrissie had taken a paper round to help eke out the family budget. Now it seemed the situation would ease with their mother's good news.

'Tell us about it, Mom,' they chorused.

'It's at George Masons up the village; the money's not too grand, but we'll manage. With two lots of wages coming in, you can give up the paper round now, luv.'

'You sure, Mom? I don't mind doing it if it helps.'

'No, you need to be here for the little ones.'

'When you starting, Ma?' Babs queried.

'Monday, I'll be so happy to leave those cleaning jobs behind. Some of those toffs don't half luk down their bloody noses at ya. I'd have a celebration for us if I could afford it,' Lily remarked. 'Tell you what, we'll all go up town when I get my first wage packet and look round the shops and markets, we ain't done that for ages, have we?'

'That'll be nice.' The girls were delighted their mom looked so happy.

'I'm off, Ma,' Babs called, making her way to the front door.

'You going to see Alan, then?' Lily tried to sound agreeable, but she strongly disagreed with her eldest child's relationship after what Alan had

The Other Place

said.

'Yes, I'll be back early though, and I'll give you a hand tomorrow. Alan's going to see his relations for the weekend.'

'What, and he's not invited you? It's about time he asked you to marry him, ain't it?' Pursing her lips Lily gave her daughter a shrewd look.

'I think Alan just accepts that we'll marry,' she said, crossing her fingers behind her back. 'There's nowhere for me to sleep at his aunt's. Bye, see you soon.' The front door slammed.

Babs seethed as she hurried down the road. Trust Lily to dig the knife in about Alan not proposing. Babs was convinced he was too scared to ask her because of what his mother would say. In his mother's eyes Babs wasn't good enough for her precious son. That's why she hadn't been invited to go with them for the weekend. It hurt Babs, but no way would she show her real feelings to her family. Even if they couldn't marry it would be lovely to be engaged.

CHAPTER 5

Lily liked her new job at the grocery store, despite it not bringing in much money. They managed; Bab's money helped. She put money aside for rent and coal, money for the other bills went into a tot on the shelf above the fireplace.

Lily had always been a good manager and a breast of lamb went a long way with a few cheap veggies. They could always have dripping or lard spread on toast if they ran short, but they never had so far and her kids would never go hungry, the little woman vowed.

'I'll work me fingers to the bones for me family,' she told anyone within earshot, 'I want the best for them. I'll prove I don't need a man to support me and mine.'

***

It felt strange to Lily returning to work after such a long break. New job, new life, new beginnings, she told herself, taking a deep breath as she opened the back door of the shop on her first day.

She was glad the women were friendly. She was soon swathed in an all-round white overall, bright blonde hair tucked under a white cap, and the shop supervisor escorted her to the cheese and bacon counter where she was to work.

The Other Place

'Phew,' she told her eldest daughter later that day as she fried some bacon bits for their tea, 'the smell of the cheese and sides of bacon nearly knocked me for six. They smell just like Alf's sweaty socks used to.'

'Did you like it, Mom?' Babs asked anxiously, getting the cutlery out for the meal.

'Yes.' Lily was sparkling. 'I did. I was worried they'd throw me out after an hour as I'm not very bright, but I got on fine with the work and the other women are really friendly; that's apart from one woman called Nan, she's a bit of a gossip and a troublemaker. Honest, Babs, you should hear what the other women told me about her.'

Babs grinned. Listening to her mom, she knew she'd be fine and settle down at the shop; she was pleased. She'd fretted all day in case she didn't like it. Relieved her mom was happy, she whitened Greg's pumps for school the following day, thinking of how lovely it would be to be married to Alan.

***

Chrissie filled the washing up bowl from the kettle and swished the plates around noisily. Her mom was helping her.

'Watch it, girl, you'll break them plates, and we can't afford new ones.' Suddenly, Lily found the words bursting from her lips, 'Why do you cry out in the night, Chrissie?'

'I didn't know I did, Mom.'

She decided to try and explain what happened

to her. Unfortunately, Lily's reaction was exactly as she had expected. As soon as she mentioned that she felt trapped in her mind, Lily exploded.

Slamming the plates in the cupboard with a clatter and shutting the cupboard door with an almighty bang, she shouted angrily,

'What do you mean, saying things like that? Only people who ain't right in their bloody heads would even think they was trapped in their mind. You'd better watch out, me gal, or people will say you're a barm pot. It's just a dream you have, that's all, you daft sod. Do you hear me?'

Lily's voice reached a crescendo; she was really frightened that if Chrissie spread this around, people would think her daughter was mad. She remembered that when she was younger, Chrissie had said a similar thing. Alf had been listening and he'd said he would deal with her another time. She wondered if Alf's actions, at shutting Chrissie in the cupboard under the stairs, had tipped her daughter over the edge. Since that night she had often heard her screaming in fear in the darkness of the night. Many times she'd tried to go to her, but Alf would pull her back, snapping, 'Leave her be, she deserves a good hiding for waking us up.' Fearing he would carry out his threat, Lily would lie down again feeling guilty that she did not go to her troubled daughter.

Yet again guilt made her reject her daughter; she couldn't risk showing her sympathy, a neighbour might find out and they'd suffer from the gossip. She turned away from her daughter and lit a cigarette, surprised to find her hands trembling.

The Other Place

Damn it, why couldn't her daughter act like a normal teenager?

'You're right, Mom. I was only joking.' Chrissie hung her head to avoid showing her disappointment. She spread the tea towel to dry on the draining board and sadly made her way upstairs to bed.

***

Chrissie felt more despondent than ever. She had no one to chat with. Amy never visited. Her mom worked. Since she'd left school, her days were full of household chores, washing, cleaning and shopping. Babs had a full-time job and other commitments. How she longed for a friend to talk to about what had happened to her. She had flashes of memory now and again and she thought perhaps it would all make sense and become clear if she had someone to confide in.

Sometimes when she took the young ones out, she felt as if someone was watching her and it made her feel very uncomfortable. This had happened to her a few times over the years. She'd never told her mother as she was certain she would scoff, telling her she was scared of her own shadow.

Since Alf had left, Lily had changed. Oh, she knew she still loved them in her own way, but little things about her irked Chrissie. Like, she never wore her wrap-around flowery pinafore anymore. Chrissie liked Lily's pinafores; they smelt of home, warmth, cakes, vegetables, coal – well, everything that made their mom the person she was. She

The Other Place

always liked cuddling her (even though she pushed her away sometimes, saying, "dun't be daft") and smelling her pinafore. Now *she* wore it, not Lily. She wore makeup and was always fiddling with her hair. Chrissie was beginning to feel old and more like a mother than a daughter. A great longing to escape from the house and be on her own for a while overcame her.

Shrugging out of her hated pinafore, she yanked her coat off the back-door nail and shouted, 'I'm off for a walk, Ma.'

'What about the dinner and the kids?' Lily walked towards her, wagging her finger. 'This is your job, Chrissie, you took it on, yer know. You promised if I let you leave school, that you'd do all the jobs for me.'

'But, Ma, I've never had a day off since you started work,' she whined.

'Well, my lady, I've never had a bloody day off in me life.' She almost spat the words out.

Replacing her coat Chrissie shuffled back to the sink, and Lily collapsed relieved onto a kitchen stool.

'See, Chris, it's like this: once you marry, that's it, you've given your life to a man, lock, stock and barrel. Once the first kid arrives, the rope begins to tighten; after the second kid, that's it, you're done for life. There's no more visits to the pictures, or nice new clothes and having your hair done. Husbands and kids is all that counts from the time you sign that marriage register. Don't forget all the bloody housework you have to do day in and day out, either; polishing furniture, windows, and

The Other Place

scrubbing floors. You remember that, me lady, before you get married and sign your whole life away.' Bitterness twisted her pretty features, and fishing her cigarettes and matches from her pocket she lit one and inhaled deeply.

At the sink Chrissie coughed on the smoke and wiped her eyes.

Risking a smack on the face from Lily, she said, 'Do you have to smoke, Ma? I hate the smell.' Nervously, she added, 'Do you have to swear so much, Mom? Only the kids are beginning to copy you.'

'Yes, and when you're older you'll know why I do both. Being married is bloody hard work, me girl, and I need me fags; and if I swear, so bloody what?'

'I'll never smoke nor swear.' Slapping the wet dishcloth on the draining board, she set about laying the table. 'I got us some nice chops from the butcher's and we've got mashed potatoes and cabbage with them. I thought they'd be nice with a bit of milk and margarine mashed in for the kids. I hope you like it, Mom.'

Lily dropped her cigarette into the saucer she was using as an ashtray, jumped up, and folded her daughter into her arms.

'I'm sorry, luv, truly I am. You're nowt but a young wench and I've been rotten to you. I've been that wrapped up in myself thinking about that bugger Alf Brown and worrying about money, I forgot about you skivvying here and never having time to yourself. You're such a good girl.' Kissing the top of her head, she gave her another hug and

The Other Place

gently pushed her into a chair, telling her firmly, 'Now, you sit there and don't move. I'll dish the dinner up, and afterwards you can have first bath for a change and go to bed and read.'

A huge grin spread across Chrissie's young face. 'Really, Ma? I got a good book from the library when I was there last week.' Wriggling on the chair to get comfortable, Chrissie realised just how tired she was. Mentioning the library she thought of how much she enjoyed her visits to it; the smell and the texture of the books gave her a thrill that she found hard to put into words. At times when she touched the book covers, it was as if the words wanted to explode right out of the book and into her head. She often wished she had more time for reading.

She wasn't sleeping well at all lately. The claustrophobic feeling persisted night after night and occasionally it even happened in the daytime. Even when she passed a telephone box, she began to feel panicky about the thought of being unable to get out of it should she have to make a call.

Gradually, the warmth of the kitchen stole around her; she could hear Lily humming an Elvis tune in the background, and her eyes became heavy. She drifted off to sleep, exhausted in mind and body, but happy remembering the hug her mom had given her. Perhaps Lily did love her and Babs as much as the others?

Lily glanced across the room at her sleeping daughter and raised a finger to her lips as Jess toddled into the kitchen, followed by Greg.

'Shush, your sister's tired. Go and wash your hands both of you, then come and have your

The Other Place

dinner. We'll let Chrissie have five minutes.'

Chrissie was terrified; the nightmare was reaching out and grabbing her. She felt as if she was going to be engulfed and trapped forever inside her head, unable to ever move or speak again. She woke with a terrified scream.

'What is it, luv?' Lily put her knife and fork down, shocked at the sight of the sheer horror on her daughter's face.

'Nothing, Mom, honest. Just a silly dream.' Shaking her head, wiping away her tears, and hoping the horror would disappear, she got up to fetch her dinner off the stove.

Once seated, she noticed her siblings eyeing her up across the table. 'What ya staring at?'

They flushed and looked down at their plates.

'I was worried about you, Chris, that's all,' Greg murmured through a forkful of mashed potato.

'Don't speak with your mouth full,' his sister retorted swiftly.

'Huh, see you're all right now,' Greg laughed.

Jessie smiled fondly across at her older sister. 'Kiss, Chris,' she said, blowing one across the table to her.

'Thank you.' She felt choked with love for her siblings. Pushing her dinner away, she got up from her chair saying, 'Ma, I'm going for a bath and then to bed. I'm not hungry tonight.'

'Tell you what, love, I'll bring you a nice cup of cocoa up later.'

Later, lying in bed, Chrissie wondered how she could control her fear. It was making her life almost impossible to cope with.

The Other Place

***

Chrissie was eighteen years old and despite still being troubled by the claustrophobic feelings, she had blossomed. The job she had been hoping for at the Co-op never materialised. Fortunately she managed to get one at a local greengrocer's and she enjoyed the work. She felt comparatively happy; by keeping busy she was more in control of her life. Nights could still be pretty horrific at times if she had a panic attack. Chrissie had discovered that by controlling her breathing, sometimes the awful feeling would leave her.

One of the neighbours had the two younger ones after school. Nothing had been seen or heard of Alf since the day he had left. The most startling news was that eighteen months after his disappearance, the police had popped round to see Lily.

The young constable had stood in the living room and dropped the bombshell.

'We know where your husband is, Mrs Brown.'

Lily's blue eyes lit up.

'Oh, where's he bin, then, and when's he coming home?' She almost started dancing with joy.

The sisters exchanged desperate looks that spoke volumes. Why did she want him back? Since he'd disappeared this was a happy home.

Shaking his head, the constable told her, 'Sorry, Mrs Brown, he says he's not coming back.'

Sitting down with a bump, her colour draining

The Other Place

from her face, she asked, 'He's not coming back, you're telling me? Now listen here, you, –'

'Ma, don't speak to the policeman like that.' Babs thought she'd better intercede before her mother landed up in a police cell. 'It's not his fault, is it?'

Smiling at Babs with a wicked twinkle in his eye, the young officer went on.

'It's fine, miss, your mother is obviously shocked at this news. As I said, Mrs Brown, I'm very sorry. The case is closed.'

'Closed? You can't close the case until he's back here where he belongs, with his wife and family.'

'I'm sorry, Mrs Brown, but Mr Brown is in good health physically and mentally. There's nothing further we can do. We're not allowed to tell you where he's residing.'

'Don't take on, Mom.' Patting her mother's hand, Babs slipped an arm around her shoulders. 'Thank you, Constable, for letting us know,' she called as Chrissie showed him to the door.

The Other Place

Chapter 6

When Chrissie James of Fellfeld, Birmingham – as yet still not on the telephone at home – was nineteen years of age, she decided to go window shopping in Birmingham City Centre. Walking down Corporation Street, she caught sight of a sign advertising a hypnotherapist/clairvoyant. Reading the notice, she saw that hypnotherapy was an extremely useful treatment to help people who experienced emotional problems. This jolted her memory as she recalled having recently read an article about it in a women's magazine. She remembered thinking how interesting it sounded. Noting that the therapist's practice wasn't far away, and as she had time to spare, she decided to make a visit.

Heading up New Street, she was tempted to go into Central Library and the museum and art gallery, but resisted as something urged her to keep going. Glancing to her right she saw the statue of Queen Victoria. She also noticed there were a lot of tourists around the Town Hall; many were feeding the pigeons outside the library in Paradise Street.

Chrissie eventually found her way to the practitioner's premises situated in a side street, not far from Bingley Hall. A small sign on the entrance door stated that Kitty Medley, Hypnotherapist/Clairvoyant, worked in room number five. What she didn't know as she walked

The Other Place

into the entrance hall was that this visit was going to be one of the most defining moments of her life.

She was surprised how spacious the entrance hall was; the walls were painted pale blue and the doors leading off the hall were painted white, lending a light, airy feeling to the space. On a side table was a beautiful vase of blue, white and lilac flowers. A notice on the facing wall directed visitors to the first floor for the hypnotherapist's practice. Climbing the wide, white-painted staircase, she thought the building had an excellent atmosphere.

Entering the reception area, she pressed the bell and sat down, expecting to wait a few minutes.

A door at the end of the room immediately swung wide open and a plump, grey-haired, elderly woman beckoned her inside.

Chrissie suddenly found herself sitting in a chair facing the woman across a highly-polished desk, who introduced herself as Kitty, asking which of her services she wanted. The woman's deep melodious voice immediately made her feel relaxed until her next words. 'And you are Chrissie.'

She was astounded and a little frightened at the woman's words. She couldn't work out how she knew her name and was ready to grab her bag and leave.

'Don't fret, sometimes we are told these things by our spirit guides.' The woman reached across her table and patted Chrissie's hand. 'I think I'll give you a free card reading first and that way we will get to know each other better.'

'I can pay,' Chrissie said, her pride to the fore.

The Other Place

'I know you can, but I feel it is right at this time that you shouldn't pay me.'

Chrissie shuffled the tarot pack and passed them to Kitty. Something told her this reading was going to be important.

The hypnotherapist looked at her cards then threw a wary look at the young girl.

She cleared her throat, after which her deep voice sounded even louder to the young woman's ears.

'For years you have suffered the most horrific feelings of claustrophobia, my love.' Patting her hand again, she lowered her voice. 'We need to speak about this, I think I may be able to help you.'

She flipped the cards together and put them away.

Shocked beyond measure at what the therapist had just told her, Chrissie asked anxiously, 'Do you really think you can help me?'

Nodding her head, the woman replied, 'I'm certain I can.'

'What can you do?'

'You might not welcome my idea, but I feel you need to find out what caused it to happen in the first place. This may well be an unpleasant experience for you to go through, but once you are able to face it, you should then be able to move on with your life. It will help you begin to heal.' Kitty's whole demeanour spoke of warmth, love and comfort, making Chrissie feel secure for the first time in years, and she eagerly accepted her offer.

Words that had long been held back for fear of ridicule poured from her lips like a torrent. 'You

The Other Place

see, for so long now I've had this awful feeling inside my head. I feel trapped inside my mind and I can't escape from it. When it happens, it's so frightening. I feel as if I'll never be able to move, speak, in fact, do anything ever again. I think I'll be trapped like it for evermore. It would be like a living death for me. That's the only way I can explain it.' Tears welled up in her eyes and she began to cry as she recalled the horror she had been going through for so many years.

Kitty reached across the desk, and with a weather-beaten hand she squeezed Chrissie's hand tightly. 'Go on, love, it will do you good to talk about it.'

'I find it so difficult to explain. When I was young, I began to feel panicky if I was in a room and the door was closed. I disliked people being too near me but I managed. When I was older, the trapped feeling started inside my head. It was awful. I couldn't escape it. I had trouble breathing, my chest hurt, I couldn't move my limbs, and I thought I'd never be able to communicate with anyone ever again. It was awful and sometimes it became almost unbearable. I was young and I just knew I couldn't explain it to anyone. My family would certainly not have understood, and I never really had any friends to talk to. I only had Amy, my imaginary friend, when I was younger, but she disappeared from my life. I've never had a friend since.'

There, she'd said it; the thing that had haunted her was completely out in the open for the first time in her life. She looked worriedly at Kitty, thinking, *What if she gets up and walks away, what will I do?* She was so concerned that the woman would think her stupid that she reached for her bag and prepared to leave.

Kitty grabbed her hand. 'Sit down, lass. You've been through a terrible time all these years, and I'm going to try and help you.'

Shuffling uncomfortably, Chrissie whispered, 'You don't think I'm daft, do you? Sometimes I think I'm going mad.'

Bobbing her head, the woman replied, 'Listen, something traumatic happened to you and, since then, you've shut it out of your mind and this has allowed it to build up to the level it has. If we can unravel the mystery, I think you will begin to be able to live with it, and who knows, you may well lose many of your fears.'

'Really?' Her green eyes opened wide as she tried to absorb what the older woman had just told her.

'Yes, Chrissie, it will help you cope. I'll also teach you how to relax and it won't be long before you are able to regress yourself.'

'That would be interesting.'

'I think the best idea is for you to come and visit me at home and we'll take it from there.' She was drawn to help this young girl. She could see how she had suffered emotional problems for most of her life. She sensed the girl needed to feel loved. She knew she would be able to help her relax far more quickly in her home.

Chrissie welcomed the invitation and quickly ascertained that, surprisingly, Kitty lived two streets

The Other Place

away from her in Fellfeld.

She scribbled down her address and they made arrangements to meet the following day as it was the therapist's day off.

Chrissie hurried off to catch the 61 bus home from Hill Street. Walking along the street, she felt as if she was being watched and glanced nervously over her shoulder. She caught sight of a young man dressed in a light-coloured coat, observing her. Realising she had spotted him, he turned and rapidly strode away. Chrissie shook her head, wondering why in the world anyone would want to watch her. Confused and worried she hurried to join the bus queue. If only she was able to share things with her family, but she simply lacked the courage to talk to her mom or her sister, and feared their scorn. They were both too busy with their own lives, anyway. She hoped whoever it was would go away. Of course, she could just be imagining someone was following her; it could be another phobia.

***

Watching the young woman depart, the therapist shook her head worriedly, making her grey curls bounce about. She knew Chrissie faced an uphill journey to sort her problems out, but she was determined to help her as much as she could.

Kitty had been a practicing hypnotherapist and clairvoyant for more years than she cared to remember; she used the cards as a means to help relax her clients and give her an insight into what

The Other Place

was happening in their lives.

Never having married, she preferred to devote her time to helping others. She was looking forward to helping the young woman. She was certain it was going to be hard for Chrissie at first, but as time passed she would definitely feel the benefit.

Knowing she could trust the young woman, she had no qualms welcoming her into her home. Kitty was ill and hoped she would be around long enough to help Chrissie through her problems.

***

'First things first.' She smiled at Chrissie the following day. 'Make yourself comfortable in front of this warm fire and I'll bring you a cup of coffee through. Do you take sugar, petal?'

'Yes please, Kitty, two spoons.'

'Glad to see you are not on a diet like a lot of today's young women.'

As she took a gulp of the sweet coffee, she sighed. 'Actually, Kitty, I would love to lose some weight, but I enjoy my food too much.' Groaning, she patted her stomach and hips.

'Get away with you, girl, you look just right. It isn't right to diet. You're tall and would look daft if you were skinny. You would look like a bean pole.'

Kitty took a sip of her tea; she had never liked the taste of coffee.

'Let's sort out what we're going to do.' She folded her plump fingers together and looked at Chrissie with her all-seeing eyes.

My goodness, Chrissie thought, *Kitty can read my*

mind. The shutters came down immediately, and the older woman chuckled. 'Yes, you'll do well. You're a natural psychic. Lift those barriers, you've already told me everything you can remember, so there's no need to try and hide anything, I'm here to help you.'

Chrissie nodded. 'I really appreciate your help, Kitty.'

'Right, now what you need to do is to relax and start counting backwards from ten. You will begin to feel tired, but there is nothing to worry about.' As Kitty counted, Chrissie relaxed and fell into a deep sleep.

***

'I'm in a village, it's surrounded by a wood and there's a crowd of young children playing. They're dressed in tatty old clothing. There's a woman calling them to go in, they're running towards her. I'm running away in the opposite direction. I'm leaving the village forever.' She sounded breathless and frightened, but she continued. 'I'm in the woods, it's beginning to get dark, it's difficult to walk. I'm a bit scared, but not as much as if I'd stayed at home. The tree branches are ripping my clothes, and the brambles are scratching my arms and legs. I'm cold and wet.' She gave a small sob.

'Take your time, love. How old are you?' Kitty patted her arm consolingly.

Breathing heavily as if she was in a trance, Chrissie's dialect changed into a country accent. 'I think I'm about nineteen or so. It's so dark in this

The Other Place

wood, but I have to get away, he said he was going to do it again when 'im and Mom came home.' Tears were running down her cheeks and she was choking back the sobs.

'Who, your dad?' Kitty's voice intruded gently.

'No, not my real dad, he's dead. I mean my step-dad, Arthur. He hates me. He thinks it's funny what 'e does. It's 'orrible and me mom laffs as well, 'e told me that if I tell anyone, he'll beat me. He's hit me before, you know. I don't know why he hates me so much as I've never done anything wrong.' Tears were falling down Chrissie's cheeks as she continued. 'There's no one to help me. I'm so alone. I have to run away. If I can find the track through the wood, it'll tek me to the village where me grandparents live.' Her voice was getting louder as she became more upset.

'Take your time and breathe deeply,' the therapist urged.

Chrissie was terribly distressed but did as Kitty said; taking some really deep breaths she relaxed into the chair with a loud sigh. Something was happening; a chink of light had appeared at the back of her mind, and she tried to enter it. It disappeared as quickly as it had appeared.

'There's a farmer up ahead, 'is smock is splattered with cow dung. He's herding his cows along the lane. They stink vile. It's milking time, see. I'm hiding behind the trees, keeping out of the way of his dogs. They're vicious devils, one of 'em bit young Barney from the village, you know, and he was only walking up the lane. The farmer knows me and 'e'll tell Ma if he sees me, then she'll come

The Other Place

looking for me and mek me go back.'

Chrissie fell silent and Kitty was worried she'd slip further back in time. Leaning over, she rubbed the girl's hands. She noticed they were red raw from washing and that her nails were bitten to the quick. *The poor girl,* she thought, filled with sorrow. 'Tell me, what's your name and what's the village called where you live?'

'My name is Ella, my village is Heayric.' Her voice was fading away.

'Relax, girl, just one more question. What's your mother's name?'

'Emily,' came the prompt reply, then she slumped in the chair.

The hypnotherapist was relieved and pleased. She had a link now and Ella's age of nineteen was very significant indeed. She was fairly certain she would be able to help her. Kitty knew that something really bad had happened to this young woman years ago, and reliving Ella's experience would hopefully help her remember what it was; only then would she be able to leave the past behind and move on with her life.

The older woman derived a great deal of satisfaction from helping other people. Living alone never worried her; after all, she had her friends from the "other side" who communicated with her. She rarely discussed this with anyone, knowing few people understood the spiritual realm.

As Chrissie was leaving, Kitty told her she was certain there was something else that had happened in her life that was holding her back. She reassured the young girl that in the fullness of time, she was

The Other Place

certain everything would turn out right for her.

'I know you say you'll never marry. You will, you know, but not until you are older and more settled. The proposal will surprise you and it will happen at "The Other Place". I know you won't believe me, but my words will return to you when it happens.'

Chrissie shook her head vehemently. 'That all sounds very mysterious, but no, Kitty,' she insisted firmly, 'I will never marry.'

She had no idea why she was so against marriage, but from a young age she had determined that it was not for her, and over the years, she had deepened her resolve.

Thinking about it, how could she marry? She hated anyone being near her. If anyone was walking behind her, she sidestepped them as fast as she could; there were so many things that would send her mind in a spin, and she couldn't understand how Kitty would think that she, Chrissie James, would ever marry.

Chapter 7

Despite all Lily's admonitions, Babs was marrying Alan at Birmingham Registry Office. They were only having a small do, but Babs was ecstatic.

'It doesn't matter to me about not having any children,' she'd informed her mother blithely. 'I'm marrying Alan cus I love him.'

'You just wait and see, my girl,' Lily had muttered darkly. 'I've told you, it ain't natural that a man don't want any kids. And what about me? I want some grandchildren.' Of course, she was fully aware of Bab's plan and knew the marriage would fall apart. 'You'll see, marriage ain't about sunshine and roses, you daft mare. You should get out, enjoy yourself, travel, do something exciting.'

Babs shrugged. 'I'm marrying the man I love and that's all there is to it.'

Lily gave up then and changed the subject.

'Have you noticed our Chrissie's been acting strangely these last few weeks?'

'No, not really, Ma, but then I've been busy with my wedding preparations, haven't I? What do you mean, acting strangely?'

'Well, sneaking off when she comes in from work. That's not like her at all.'

'Mmm, perhaps she's got a boyfriend at long last and wants to keep him to herself.'

'You could be right. I hope she has. It'll stop her thinking about all this psychic stuff. It gets on me nerves, you know, when 'er starts. She takes after your gran, a head full of ghosts and speaking to the dead. Just talking about it gives me the bloody creeps, Babs.'

Babs laughed aloud. 'It's harmless, Mom, and after all, our gran does a lot of good around her area. She's helped lots of people, not just ladies either. She's had men visit her for readings as well, and you know that blokes are normally very sceptical about that sort of thing. I wish she'd give me a reading.'

'Now don't you go pestering your gran, do you hear me? She's getting old and has more than enough to do.'

'No, I won't, Mom, but she's never given me or any of us a reading, has she?'

'No, and I doubt if she ever will. She's always said it's wrong to read for family members. Anyway, I've never wanted one. It ain't right, let the dead rest in peace, that's my motto. It's wrong to disturb them.'

Raising her eyebrows, Babs thought, *Here we go again!* She'd heard it many times before. 'I only want a reading for my future, Ma. I don't want to communicate with the dead.'

'What will be, will be, Babs,' Lily thundered on like a steam engine. 'If it's going to happen, it will, knowing about it won't change it, you know. And another point, disturbing the dead can lead to very bad things happening; you just don't know what you're stirring up.'

'I'd still like to know what me future holds,' Babs muttered under her breath as she fished for her white stiletto-heeled shoes from the cupboard under the stairs. She always felt classy when she wore them.

'I'm just going to give me shoes a quick wipe over, and then I'm off to meet Alan. Whoops, I mean "my" not "me". I've got to learn to speak proper. Are me stocking seams straight, Mom?'

Lily gave a nod, followed by a grunt, and shrugged her slim shoulders. 'Well, I'm still wondering what our Chrissie's up to and hope her ain't involved in all this ghostly stuff, that's all.' With that, she went off to mix the ingredients for a Spotted Dick pudding.

***

Chrissie James was indeed really mixed up with all the ghostly stuff.

Sitting in Kitty's small room, sipping her coffee and watching the play of light from the fire, she knew that soon she would slip back into Ella's lifetime. This didn't worry her at all; despite feeling every emotion that Ella experienced, she knew that in the end it would help her come to terms with her life and hopefully help her move on. She trusted Kitty implicitly; she felt safe and secure in her company.

How strange, she thought pensively, *it's as if Ella and I are leading parallel lives, but I'm Ella, and she's me. But what happened to me in the past?* The chink of light at the back of her mind was still there, but for some reason it seemed it wasn't the right time to delve any deeper into it.

The Other Place

Thinking about it, Ella had been a happy little girl just as Chrissie had once been, but Ella had run away from home because something had frightened her, just as something appeared to have frightened Chrissie. The chink of light brightened for a second as the thought chased through her head. *Should I leave home?*

Shaking her head, she knew she couldn't leave her mother and the youngsters; no, she had to stay put until the children were older and independent. *I'll be old then, but what will be will be. I have to help Mom.*

Taking a deep breath she glanced at the therapist and smiled.

'Thank you for helping me, I really do appreciate it.'

'Go on with you. It's my pleasure. I like helping people, and I hope we can get to the bottom of it all for you.' She crossed her fingers hoping against hope she would be around long enough to help the young woman. 'All you have to do is relax and start counting backwards from ten.'

***

The warmth of the fire stole over Chrissie as she settled herself comfortably in the armchair. Tucking her long legs under her skirt, she started counting backwards; the firelight played across her eyes, and she felt as if she was slipping down the longest helter-skelter she had ever been on.

***

The Other Place

The cottage was invitingly warm; slipping her thin shawl from around her slim shoulders, Ella hurried to the wood fire, thrusting her hands out towards its golden glow.

'Shall I throw some wood on, Gran?'

'Yes, we have plenty. Your granddad chopped an old ash tree down last week and we've got a good stock in. He's going to make some chairs and walking sticks from it.'

Gingerly picking up a small amount of wood from the side of the hearth, Ella quickly threw it into the fire. The flames licked around the wood, sending bright sparks spitting and shooting onto the hearth. Ella watched, mesmerised, as the smoke spiralled up the chimney. She often had the strange thought that smoke travelled on and on into different worlds that they knew nothing about. In fact, Ella had a very vivid imagination; she had made up stories all her life and had shared many of them with the village children.

'I got some water from the well for you, Gran.'

'Ta, luv, you're a good girl. You know, the ash tree has always been known for its healing qualities.'

'Really, Gran?' Ella enjoyed listening to her gran's stories.

Nodding her head, 'Yes, folklore says if a child with a broken limb goes through a split ash tree, he will be healed.'

'That's interesting. I wonder if it's true. You know, Gran, a gypsy came to our house last year and reckoned she could tell the future from looking

The Other Place

into the fire.'

'I've heard that before,' her gran called across the room, as she unwrapped a loaf of bread from a piece of damp cloth and proceeded to cut thick slices ready for the soup she'd made for their meal. 'Put that pot of soup on the range for a minute, Ella, and give it a good stir. Did the gypsy tell your mom's fortune for her?'

'No, Mom hid from her, she was scared. Mom says she doesn't hold with the gypsy fortune-tellers or any of that funny stuff they talk about.'

'Conny?' Tom, her husband, came into the room. 'Is dinner ready?' he asked, glancing round the small family room.

'Yes, it's soup today with some bread and there's a bit of cheese to follow for a change. I did some work up at the big house. The cook sent word asking me to go up and help her out. She gave me some butter, cheese and eggs in exchange.' She smiled broadly, thinking she'd done well out of the deal. 'What's more, she's offered both of us work and will give us food *and* pay us a few coppers. How about that, Tom Earnwell? With that money and the bit from your carpentry work, we'll manage the winter months now.'

He grinned, pleased at her words. Tom had been worried about feeding young Ella. Work was short in the country at this time of the year and having an extra mouth to feed was an added worry. Not that he begrudged his favourite granddaughter anything. He'd go without food himself rather than see her or his Conny go hungry.

'That's good. I'm glad. You'll be inside in the

warmth, won't you?'

She nodded, stirring the soup.

'That's a blessing, I don't want you working outside in the cold and wet,' he remarked, casting a fond glance at his wife.

After taking his boots off, he washed himself in the bowl of water that Conny had left ready for him. He would have sluiced himself off outside, but his wife wouldn't let him during the cold months.

When he was seated at the table, Conny smiled at her granddaughter.

'Fetch the soup over, Ella, there's a duck. Yes, Tom, I'm relieved about the work. It'll be a big help. Winter's always a worrying time of the year for the likes of us who work the land, but we'll be able to manage this year, thank goodness.' She poured him a generous helping and shared the remainder between Ella and herself.

Ella was feeling better now that she was away from the immediate threat of her evil parents. She knew she couldn't stay with her grandparents for long, but at least for the time being she was safe.

'I'll only stay for a week or so, Gran,' she told Constance.

'You don't have to rush off, child. I mean, where can you go?'

'I'm going to try and find work cleaning or something.' She tried to put a sparkle in her voice but failed miserably.

'You'll be fine,' her grandfather reassured her, breaking his bread into the vegetable soup.

'Nice soup, Conny, the cheese will finish it off nicely.'

The Other Place

'Thanks, Tom.' She smiled lovingly across the table at her husband. Despite never having much, they had always managed and Conny realised how lucky she was to have married such a good, steady man.

'I've always wanted to be a nursemaid in a big house.' The words were out before Ella could stop them.

Tom sliced himself a hunk of cheese and put it on a thick slice of the crusty bread. Chomping on the food, he cast his granddaughter a quizzical look.

'Now then, lassie.' Swallowing hard, he gulped his tea down and wiped his mouth with the back of a gnarled hand. 'Look, you're better than a nursemaid, you know.' Tom had always secretly favoured Ella out of all his grandchildren. He thought her the most intelligent and he wanted her to do well. Always a sensitive soul, he knew that something had badly frightened her at his daughter's house. He had a strong suspicion of what had happened and wanted to get her away from the area as soon as possible. *If she goes to Birmingham as a nursemaid, she'll just be given menial jobs,* he thought. He didn't want that for his special girl, she deserved better.

'There's nothing else I can do, unless I become a tweeny, Granddad,' Ella said plaintively.

'You're not going to be a scullery maid, they're treated very badly. You underestimate yourself, child. Listen to me; for years, you've been telling the village children your stories, haven't you?'

'Why, yes.' Finishing her tea, she was puzzled as she explained, 'They're just stories I've made up.'

The Other Place

'Well, then, I don't know how I'm going to do this, but if I work it out, you'll have a far better job than domestic work.' He gave her a huge wink and removed himself to his armchair, where he contentedly stretched his mud-spattered trouser legs out towards the fire and fell asleep.

Ella looked at her grandmother, perplexed. 'I wonder what he means, Gran.'

'I don't know, but let's clear this away. Happen he'll tell us when he's had his five minutes.'

They cleared the table and washed up the dishes.

'There's your ale, Tom,' Conny said. 'For goodness sake, tell us your idea for our granddaughter.' She took her darning out. Ella sat on the floor beside her, feeling warm and loved.

Taking a huge swig of his ale, Tom looked fondly at Ella and his wife.

'Hear me out, both of you,' he said sternly, beetling his shaggy eyebrows. 'I've been giving this a lot of thought as I had my suspicions our Ella would eventually leave home. Well, truth to tell, the idea has been in the back of my mind for a long time and now seems to be the right time to tell you about it.'

'Come on then, man, spit it out, we want to know what it is. Ouch!' Conny sucked her finger. She'd just stabbed herself with the darning needle.

'You all right, Gran?' Ella knelt in front of her, took a piece of clean rag from her apron pocket and, dabbing her gran's finger, chuckled. 'I think you'll survive.'

'Cheek,' Conny laughed. 'Tom Earnwell, if you

don't tell us this minute what you're planning, I'll chase you all the way into Birmingham on the end of my broom.'

After they'd all stopped laughing Tom lit his old clay pipe, and after a couple of puffs to make sure it was going, he gave them both a serious look.

'Here's what I've been thinking.'

Watching the pipe smoke swirling around, she missed her granddad's first words. 'Sorry, Granddad, what did you say?'

'I think you should get yourself a little storytelling business going.' Clamping his pipe tightly between his teeth, he cleared his throat and looked at their astounded faces.

Ella's green eyes opened wide, as did her generous mouth. She simply stared at him in amazement. Conny dropped her darning and was looking at him as if she couldn't believe her ears.

'Look,' he said gruffly, 'I know it sounds impossible – anything new always does – but our granddaughter has a wonderful talent and she can exploit it. Now I'm thinking she could be the first home storyteller. Just think on. Some of these rich folks would love to laud it around that their children had a storyteller visiting them once a week. Word would soon spread, believe me, and you'd be employed every day of the week if you wanted to be, my girl. I bet you'd be invited to bigger events as well.'

The women were sitting looking awestruck at his words. The firelight spread a rosy glow across their faces and Tom thought proudly how attractive they looked.

The Other Place

'But Granddad, my stories aren't educational,' Ella managed to stutter.

'I've listened to them, young lady, and I agree they're not educational as such, but they always have a fine moral thread running through them, and that's what people want to hear. The rich folk won't expect you to educate their children, but if you can keep them entertained for a while, they'll keep asking you back. The adults will enjoy them as well. You wait and see. You'll never run out of different stories to tell them, I know.'

Constance, who had remained silent throughout this discussion, suddenly broke in. 'I think that's a wonderful idea, Tom, I really do. It will be a real step up the ladder for our Ella.' Looking thoughtful, she continued, 'She'll need decent clothes, and how are we going to get the word around without someone else stealing the idea?'

'For a start, no one else has Ella's talents, do they? She'll only have to get her foot in one door and, believe me, these people will all be after her. Remember, I've worked at the big houses in my time, and the owners don't like to think someone else has got a stride on them. What do you think, Ella?'

Eyes sparkling, Ella looked thrilled. 'Yes, I would love to try – but Gran's right, I haven't any decent clothes, and where would I live?'

'Don't worry about clothes,' Tom reassured her. 'I have a bit of money put by for emergencies. As for where you'll live, I know someone in Birmingham who would be only too happy to let you have a couple of rooms that they rent out.

The Other Place

You'll have to provide for yourself, but I know you'll cope. They're perfectly respectable people. You'll have to live in the city, my love, near the big houses, so you can get to work easy. You're a sensible girl and I know you'll be a success.'

'That's provided it turns out for you.' Conny thought she'd better offer a word of caution. 'But if it doesn't you can always come back to us.'

'Yes, but, Gran, it's a wonderful idea that Granddad's thought up. I would never ever have thought of it.'

'Let's sleep on it, shall we?' Tom proposed, heaving himself up from his chair.

After damping the fire down, Constance kissed Ella goodnight and followed her husband into their small bedroom.

Whispering far into the night, Tom told his wife how he had planned what to do if Ella ever ran away from her wicked parents. He had long suspected them of mistreating her. He was more than proud that she had found the courage to leave. He couldn't accept that her mother knew what was happening but refused to do anything about it.

'How any daughter of mine could put that scum before her own daughter is beyond me. She's made her bring that brood of youngsters up while she's lazed around, and then to let that man do what he did for so long is diabolical.' Tom had a very good idea of what had been happening to his granddaughter back at the village. 'Once Ella is safe, I'll be paying them lot a visit.'

'Oh, Tom, no. Let sleeping dogs lie,' Constance begged, terrified what might happen to him.

The Other Place

'Don't fret, lass, I'll be taking plenty of support with me when I go,' he said.

They clung to each other for warmth and comfort until they finally fell asleep.

***

With the old cottage only having two rooms, Ella knew she couldn't stay with her grandparents for long. Tossing and turning on the straw mattress, she couldn't settle. She liked her granddad's idea, but the thought of moving to the big city disturbed her greatly. She was determined to be independent and to make her own way in the world, but realised that once she left there would be no turning back and she made her mind up that she was going to be a success in whatever she did. She was going to show her stepfather that he had no hold over her whatsoever.

She got up and peered out of the tiny window. Seeing the full moon riding high in the sky, crossing her fingers she made a wish that her future dreams would come true; hearing mice scurrying about, she hurried to snuggle back under the quilt her grandmother had lovingly stitched through the long winter nights especially for her. Ella felt warm and loved beneath its softness; as if her grandmother was holding her tightly in her arms.

As she slept, she saw herself standing in a busy street in front of a large detached house; a tall, good-looking man was standing in the doorway. On seeing her, he gave her a wide, cheeky smile, removed his hat and beckoned her to him. He asked her business and she told him she wanted to see the lady of the house; after hearing her request, he escorted her into the house. She awoke with a smile knowing the man in her dream was going to be important to her future.

***

Chrissie opened her eyes and looked at Kitty, who was watching her, a smile playing around her generous mouth.

'We'll have a cup of tea,' she announced, but seeing the girl wrinkle her nose, she added, 'all right, I'll make you a cup of coffee, then, but we'd better be quick, your mother will wonder what you're up to.'

Nodding in agreement, Chrissie followed her into the small kitchen. She liked being in Kitty's house as she never closed the intervening doors. She hated being in a room with the door closed. She always felt threatened, trapped, and she needed an escape route. It was a horrid feeling and it was difficult at times as she could never tell people how she felt. Even on cold winter days she had to slide the window open on the bus, much to the annoyance of anyone sitting near her. If Lily or Babs was with her, she would pretend she had travel sickness and then feel guilty for lying about it. She prayed she wouldn't have a panic attack while they were with her, she knew she would die of embarrassment if that happened. Strangely, foggy days helped her when she was out and about as she couldn't see people around her. Finding

Kitty to talk to had lifted the huge burden she had carried.

She found Kitty to be a warm, loving, motherly person, someone who she could tell her intimate secrets too; she knew she would never be judgemental. At times she wished with all her heart that she lived with Kitty in her snug warm house.

'What happened felt so real, it was as if I was really living in that time. I'm convinced the girl Ella is me in a previous lifetime.'

With her back to the girl, Kitty turned her head. 'Best not think about it for now, love, we haven't time to chat. Drink your coffee and take yourself home to your ma.'

Chrissie was surprised she didn't want to chat, but thought she was probably feeling tired after spending so much time helping her. After all, it was an extraordinary thing to have happened, somehow slipping back in time to another place. *It was almost like watching a film, and I was in it.* Not that it was anything like *'Gone with the Wind'*, which she had seen a few times. How she had liked that film and envied Scarlet O'Hara's confidence. It was difficult for her to grasp exactly what happened when she became Ella. Was she Ella or not? Had she really lived another life? How extraordinary the last couple of hours had been.

After Chrissie left, Kitty took some painkillers and went to bed. The pain in her stomach was extremely bad today and she knew another visit to the doctor was imminent.

***

The Other Place

'I'm back, Ma.'

'Where've you been, our Chris?' Lily remonstrated, wiping her wet hands on her apron. She didn't wear pinafores anymore as she considered them old-fashioned. Now she wore pretty embroidered aprons to keep her skirt clean.

Chrissie was astonished at how young her mom looked since Alf had left. Her hair was always nicely styled, she wore make-up most days, and she smiled a lot; Lily had lost the careworn look she had when Alf Brown had been around. She didn't slouch around in old clothes anymore, she was always smartly dressed.

Not giving her daughter time to reply, she carried on. 'You know, Chris, Alf would never have stood for you sloping off like you do,' Lily remarked.

'Nothing to do with him what I do, he's not my dad. Anyway, Mom, Alf hasn't been around for years so what's brought this on?'

She was surprised to see a flush come to her mom's face.

'You ain't seen him?' Chrissie cried, fear clutching at her stomach. 'Please don't say he's coming back here.'

'Don't be stupid. Course I ain't seen him. It's just that Mrs Smith from the bottom of the road said as she'd sin a man who looked like Alf driving a big posh black car along the Bristol Road when she was waiting for the bus, and he was dressed up to the nines looking really well to do.'

''Er's daft, then,' the worry making her speech

The Other Place

revert to her Brook Land days. 'What would 'e be doing driving a big posh car? Oh, I suppose 'e could be a chauffeur.'

'No.' Taking her cigarettes from her pocket, her mother explained, 'He wasn't dressed as a chauffeur.' Finding her box of matches empty, she ripped a narrow strip from last night's paper and put it in the fire to light her cigarette.

'You'll burn your eyebrows and hair off one of these days, Ma,' Chrissie giggled. 'Anyway,' she shrugged, 'it probably wasn't Alf she saw. Blimey, there's any number of blokes that look like him.'

Lily headed into the kitchen, followed closely by her daughter.

'I'm just going to put my things up in my room then I'll come and help you with dinner,' she told her mother as she opened the door that led from the kitchen upstairs to the bedrooms.

'Ta, luv.' Lily was quite excited wondering whether Mrs Smith had really seen Alf. *There's no one else who could look like Alf,* she mused happily, walking round the kitchen planning the dinner as she wiped the surfaces down. Lily had always been scrupulously clean.

Lily took a piece of fish from the cold slab in the pantry and, grabbing the pan of sliced chips that she'd prepared earlier, she turned the heat up under the chip-pan on the cooker.

'I'll get Chrissie to do the bread and butter,' she muttered to no one in particular. Truth to tell, she had gone on automatic pilot wondering about Alf driving a posh car. How on earth he could afford something so luxurious was beyond her.

The Other Place

***

Chrissie sat on the side of the bed. She was glad Lily had been distracted by Mrs Smith's news. It had taken the pressure off any awkward questions she might have asked her as to where she'd spent the afternoon, then what would she have said? Lily had no time for psychic phenomena of any description, and Chrissie didn't want to cause an argument, but on the other hand, she didn't want to tell lies.

Her stomach gurgled as the smell of frying chips drifted upstairs. No doubt about it, her mom was the best cook in the world.

She quickly went downstairs to see if she could help.

'You know what?' Lily's voice interrupted her thoughts.

'What, Ma?'

'For once I'd like to know me future. I'd love to know if it was Alf driving the car. In fact, I've a good mind to see a fortune-teller and have my future told.'

She was stunned. Was Lily actually asking her about having a reading? From as early as she could remember, her mom had been against fortune-tellers, yet now she was saying she wanted to go and have a reading.

Knowing Babs had secretly been teaching herself to read the playing cards, she was tempted to tell her, but thought she'd better have a word with her first.

'Erm, I think I know someone, Mom. I'll let you know.'

'Get away with you, Chris. Do you think I'm stupid? I know our Babs 'as been learning herself to read them there cards.' She gave a snort. 'You girls must think I'm barmy or something if ya thinks I dunno know what's going on under me nose.' To her astonishment Lily had slipped back into Brook Land speech.

Chrissie worried, then realised of course that Lily didn't know everything or she would certainly have been banned from seeing Kitty.

'I've heard Babs is pretty good at reading the cards.'

'I'll ask her, but then your gran always said it's wrong to read for family members.'

'You can try, Mom. If Babs is happy to read for you, there's no harm.'

***

Later that night they sat at the drop-leaf dining-room table.

Lily, with the usual cigarette in her hand, nervously tapped the table with her other hand.

'You sure this is safe, Babs?'

'Of course it is, Mom. Do you think I'd do anything wrong?' Babs chuckled. 'I ain't into giving bad messages out, you know. I only use nice cards. I'm not invoking bad spirits.'

'I can read the tarot cards, Mom,' Chrissie chimed in; she had also secretly been studying the cards for a couple of years.

'You what?'

'I said I can read the tarot cards.'

'Whatever next,' the girls' mother groaned, 'one reading the playing cards and the other reading the tarot cards. You kept that secret from me well, our Chris. Was ever a mother so blessed? Blimey, we could start our own fortune-telling business.'

Shuffling the cards, Babs passed them to Lily. 'Shuffle and cut, Mom, then pass them back to me.'

Wrinkling her nose, cigarette stuck between her lips, Lily shuffled the cards, saying, 'It's not that I believe in this sort of thing, you understand.' She gasped, coughing on her cigarette smoke.

Spreading the cards on the polished surface of the table, Babs studied them carefully.

Her mother watched her daughter's face. She was very wary about all this "funny business" as she called it, but she really wanted to find out if Alf was coming back to her. She wouldn't have him back, oh no, but she wanted to know why he'd left her, and what he'd been up to, and if it was him driving a posh car.

Bab's expression never altered as she looked at the card spread.

'All looks fine to me, Ma,' she announced cheerily, gathering them up and reshuffling the pack.

'Hey, come on, you,' Lily protested. 'You can tell me more. I wanna know what's going on with Alf.'

'I can't see him in your cards, Ma. I can see other people, men and women, but not Alf. The cards aren't good at distinguishing different people,

The Other Place

you know.'

'Get your tarot cards out, Chris. Babs is hiding summat from me, I know she is.' Lily lit yet another cigarette and watched, sharp-eyed, as Chrissie reached for her cards.

After shuffling them, Lily watched keenly as her middle daughter spread them on the table in rows of seven.

Chrissie was extremely worried at what she saw in her reading and glanced slant-eyed at Babs.

'I can see ya looking at her, Chrissie,' Lily remonstrated. 'It's my reading, not hers. Tell me the truth. What can you see?'

Babs nodded at her sister to tell their mother, knowing they couldn't hide it from her.

'Okay, Mom,' she started, swallowing hard, 'I can see Alf visiting you, and he'll be telling you some important news. I would suggest you think very carefully about any offers he'll be putting to you.'

She scooped the cards together and returned them to the box.

'Is that all you're gonna tell me?' Lily shrieked, jumping up from her chair.

'Yes, Mom, apart from the fact that I did see you'll be given a lot of money sometime soon.'

Just then, there was a loud knocking on the adjoining neighbouring wall.

'Wonder what the matter with Mrs Bower is.' The next-door neighbour was a widow of some twenty-one years. She lived alone and was inclined to nerves.

Leaving the girls to it, Lily made certain she had

The Other Place

her matches and cigarettes and made her way next door.

'Blimey, our Chrissie, it ain't looking particularly rosy for us two, is it?'

Babs looked despondent, but then a grin split her face. 'Think Mother is in for a big shock.' Both girls fell about laughing at the thought of Lily's reaction when she met up with Alf again.

Wiping the tears of laughter away, the girls looked at each other, and then started laughing again.

'Oh, I've got the stitch. Babs, pack it up, will you. After all, we ain't got much to laugh about, have we?'

'Yes, but she wouldn't have believed it if we'd told her, would she? It does mean huge changes for us two and the youngsters, doesn't it?'

'There's nothing we can do to alter it. Best we tidy up before Mom comes back.' Chrissie felt depressed after seeing what lay ahead for her and Babs. The youngsters would be all right, she was certain, but the next few months or so were going to be quite difficult for her and Babs.

Packing the fortune-telling cards away, she sighed, knowing what would be would be.

'Jess is going to look lovely as my flower girl. Sure you don't want to be my bridesmaid, Chris?'

Shaking her head, she answered, 'No, honest, I'm too shy to dress up in front of other people. You're not offended?' She had a horror of being in the limelight, apart from which she thought she would look ridiculous dressed as a bridesmaid.

'No, I'm not. I can't wait for next Saturday to

The Other Place

arrive, and then I'll be an old married woman.' Babs was so relieved that Alan had finally plucked up courage late last year and proposed to her. He had told his mother, who had raised all sorts of objections, but there was little she could do about it as he and Babs were over twenty-one so Alan could legally marry her without asking anyone's permission.

'It will be lovely, and I hope you and Alan have a very happy life together.'

She gave Babs a hug. 'Go and get ready for bed, and I'll get the cocoa ready for when Mom comes back from next door.'

Chrissie made her way into the kitchen to put the kettle on, hoping against hope her mother would choose the right road to travel when their errant stepfather finally put in an appearance. She was pleased not to be dependent on him. *I'll show him,* she declared, listening to the kettle beginning to whistle on the stove. *I'll be making my own way in the world if Alf Brown comes back on the scene. There's no way I'll ever live in the same house as him again. I'll be so successful he'll be green with envy.*

***

'How have you been, Chrissie? Not seen you for a few days.' Kitty rattled the poker in the ever-present fire. 'It keeps the water nice and hot for me,' she remarked. 'It's so nice not having to keep boiling saucepans and kettles of water to fill the tin bath.' The truth of it was, since falling ill, she felt the cold badly. Even on the hottest days she felt cold, and now tiredness was adding to her problems.

'Yes, filling tin baths seems like a hundred years ago nowadays, but really it's not so long ago. Do you know, I'd forgotten. Funny how quickly we accept change. You always have a nice fire going, Kitty, it throws out a lovely cosy heat. I know it sounds daft, but it always feels different to ours at home.'

'Might be because you've normally got the fireguard round because of Jessica and for airing the washing.'

'True.' Chrissie nodded, her eyes already feeling heavy as she stared into the flames; she started counting backwards from ten.

Kitty was surprised how quickly Chrissie had learned to hypnotise herself. Kitty had made her promise only to do it while she was around. 'You have to have someone experienced with you for a few weeks in case anything should go wrong,' she explained.

Chrissie accepted this. In fact she was pleased about it as it meant she could still visit Kitty.

***

Crossing the road carefully so as to avoid treading in the piles of horse manure littering the road, Ella ensured she avoided the stylish carriages that were going about their daily business of taking their mistresses into Birmingham to shop and visit the coffee houses. She lifted her skirt so the filth from the road and pavement didn't dirty the hem.

The Other Place

Standing at the bottom of five steps that led up to an elegant detached house, Ella wondered if she could really work in such a luxurious environment as this house seemed to be offering. Her eyes travelled over the beautifully painted red front door with its huge shining brass door knocker. There were bay windows adorned by beautiful green velvet curtains. Large flower pots placed either side of the door added to the elegant welcome.

Suddenly, the door swung wide and a stylishly dressed young man stepped outside. Catching sight of Ella, he stopped, removed his hat and beckoned her up the steps.

With a bow and a cheeky grin, he asked, 'Are you lost, young lady? May I assist you?'

Flushing to the roots of her hair, she stuttered, 'Is this the residence of Mr and Mrs Philpott?' For a moment Ella thought she recognised the young man; the name Edward quickly followed by Eddie sprang into her mind. Shaking her head she told herself not to be so stupid – where could she possibly know this young man from?

'Indeed it is.' Raising his eyebrows, Edward immediately fell hopelessly and irrevocably in love with the green-eyed, beautiful girl with honey-blonde hair who was standing in front of him.

From the sight of the curls peeping from her dark-red bonnet, to the tips of her highly polished black boots, everything about her told him she was the one for him.

He felt as if he was drowning in the sea-green depths of her eyes. Edward knew beyond a shadow of doubt that this girl would one day be his wife.

The Other Place

He had been waiting for her all his life.

'Excuse me, sir, is there something wrong?' Her voice cut through his reverie.

She was in awe of this tall, dark, handsome man and was instantly attracted to him. Common sense quickly prevailed and she was aware he would never look at the likes of her. Would he?

'Er, no.' He escorted her through the front door into a huge oak-panelled hall that simply took Ella's breath away.

'Now, if you will give me your name and who it is you are visiting, I'll call the maid. By the way, I'm the eldest son of the house, Edward, but known as Eddie to one and all.'

Oh, my goodness, somehow she did know him, but how?

He dropped his silver-handled walking stick into its depository and took aim with his hat, which landed on a hook on a highly polished hat stand a few feet away - much to her amusement.

'My name is Ella Earnwell. I'm here to see Mrs Lucy Philpott, sir,' she said quietly, eyes downcast. Her flushed cheeks belied her apparent composure.

How he longed to gaze once again into those delightful green eyes.

'Oh, you're here to see Mamma.' He gave her a quizzical look as he called, 'Polly, come here. We have a visitor to see Mamma.'

Immediately, the sound of footsteps could be heard running upstairs, and a young girl suddenly appeared framed in the narrow doorway leading into the hall. The girl was tiny, her dark hair squashed tightly under a white mob cap. She wore a long, high-necked black dress covered by a white, frilly-edged apron.

'Sir?' she queried breathlessly.

'Please tell my mother Miss Earnwell has arrived.'

Bobbing a deep curtsy, the maid scurried off down the wide hallway.

Chapter 8

Lily nearly collapsed when she heard the door knocker rattle. Although she'd been expecting it, hearing the familiar rat-tat-tat Alf had always used when he'd forgotten his door key made her heart beat faster. The night before, she'd had very little sleep worrying and wondering why she had agreed to see him.

Repeatedly, during the last few weeks, she had questioned herself as to why she wanted to see him again. Did she still love him? Despite being asked out a number of times over the preceding years by various men, she'd always refused. Lily had told herself, with two failed marriages behind her there was no room for a third.

She'd worked hard to bring her family up and reckoned she was doing a good job. The rent was paid regularly on the dot, there was always food on the table, and so what if in the past they had worn second-hand clothes from the rag market? They had never been in debt.

Things were all right. Babs was married and Chrissie was working. Greg and Jess were happily settled at school. She had her job. No, she certainly didn't need a man in her life. Did she?

They were all doing well and seemed content. So why had she done her hair and put her best skirt and blouse on, and why was her heart racing like a teenager on a first date?

The Other Place

She had sent Jessica out with the two girls, and Greg was around at his friends. There was no way Alf was going to swagger back in here and get his hands on her kids.

The door knocker rattled again.

Opening it, she hardly recognised the smart-suited figure of her husband standing in the porch.

'Hello, Lily girl, you're looking good.'

Swallowing hard in disbelief, she demanded, 'What do you want, Alf, cus if you think you can waltz in here and take my kids away from me after all these years, you're mistaken. You're acting just like the other varmint who tried it on with me years ago.' Her blue eyes flashed angrily.

'Come on, Lil, it wasn't all that long ago really.'

'You think you can walk out on me for over seven years and then stroll back in as if nothing had happened?' She was incredulous, arms folded across her slim body barring his entrance. 'I think you'd better go back to whoever you've been dossing down with, Alf Brown.'

His face took on a hard expression and he took a step towards her.

Lily felt threatened, but stood her ground. 'You ain't coming here to wreck my life again, Alf Brown, so there.'

He gave her his most winning smile. 'Now, Lil, I haven't come to take the kids away or to move back in with you. I just want to talk, but not on the porch. Do you really want all the neighbours to hear our business?'

She glanced over his shoulder and saw a small group of women on the green casting surreptitious

The Other Place

glances in their direction.

'Nosy cows,' she muttered, 'you'd better come in, then, but don't think you're getting your feet under my table ever again, Alfred Brown.' She motioned him inside with a jerk of her head.

Alf looked around the living room. Clean and neat as a new pin, he could never fault Lily on her housewifely skills, but how poor it all looked to his eyes now. Comparing this little house to his mansion, well, there was no comparison at all.

'Where's our Jessica and Greg?' he asked, sitting himself down in one of the old armchairs.

'Ain't that just typical of you, Alf Brown? Ask after your own, but ignore the other two who've been working hard to help keep them all these years you've bin away.'

He had the grace to look shamefaced. 'I'm sorry, Lil. How are the girls?' Not that he gave two hoots, really, but he wanted to smooth his way back into Lily's affections.

'Our Babs got married last week, but she's come to visit me; her and Chrissie have took Jessica out to Fellfeld Park and Greg's at his friends. Of course, Babs and Alan have their own flat in Selly Oak.' She sighed. 'I suppose Chrissie will be the next one to go.'

Alf's eyes gleamed at the thought.

'Come on, spit it out, what do ya want? I ain't got all day, you know. What you here for?'

'Well, Lily, if you remember, when I left you we hadn't been getting on all that well.'

'We was no worse than any other couple I know.'

The Other Place

'I know, but it just got too much for me and I took off. I needed to sort myself out, and I lived rough for a long time doing any sort of work I could get, but gradually I began to make a bit of money. I found a good accountant and followed his advice; it turned out to be excellent – I invested it in the car industry.'

'You invested it?' Her eyes widened in astonishment at the thought of anyone, let alone Alf, having enough money left at the end of the week to invest. Alf get lucky? He could never even find the ball in the *Birmingham Mail's* Spot the Ball contest.

'I did, and for once in my life, I came up trumps. I thought if I make good, Lily will be proud of me and have me back.' He flushed as he explained, 'I am an extremely rich man, Lily. I own my own house, three cars; well you name it, I own it.'

For the first time in her life, Lily was dumbstruck. She collapsed into the nearest chair with a thump. She stared at him, not knowing whether to believe him or not. After a few seconds, she spoke.

'You're a daft sod, Alf Brown, you shud have known that you could come home. We only had a row.'

He took his leather wallet out and showed her photographs of a beautiful house standing in its own grounds. It looked wonderful.

'You own this, Alf?'

'I do, lass,' he said. 'Would you like to come and see it, Lil?'

The Other Place

'You wanna take me there?' she squeaked, hardly believing her ears.

'I would like to take you now if you'll come.'

This didn't sound at all like the Alf she knew, and she was uncertain what to do. With all her heart, she wanted to go with him.

'Is it far, Alf?'

'About ten minutes or so in me car; please come with me, Lily.' He stretched out his hand beseechingly. She noticed how clean his nails were. She remembered how dirty they had always been when they lived together. A sure sign, she thought, of his improved lifestyle, along with his expensive clothes.

She ignored his hand, not wanting to give him any encouragement in that department. She wondered why he wanted her to see the house and didn't think it was to show off; maybe it was for old times' sake.

Making a snap decision, she scribbled a note for the girls to say she wouldn't be long, grabbed her coat from the back door and followed Alf to his car.

The women on the green watched in amazement as Lily climbed into Alf's shiny black Austin limousine. She couldn't help feeling a little smug as she snuggled onto the bench seat alongside him. She'd never been in a car before! Now she was sitting beside her husband in his car, it felt good.

Soon they were cruising along the Bristol Road towards Rednal. Lily was awestruck by the sheer luxury of the car. Alf took a sudden turn and she slid across the polished leather seat, landing beside him; blushing furiously, she quickly slithered back to her own side.

'You could have stayed beside me, you know!' Alf cast a cheeky look to where she was sitting as close to the door as possible. He shrugged his shoulders when she ignored him. 'Nearly there, Lil – you're going to enjoy this, I know.'

***

He sped along a narrow country lane, turned into a wide, tree-lined driveway, and pulled up outside a large detached house. 'Blimey, it's a bloody mansion house,' Lily spluttered in shock. It was the one she had seen in the photograph!

'Sorry, the front entrance is being worked on, unfortunately we'll have to use the back entrance for today.' He led her down the side of the house, and following the path they walked past borders of late-flowering chrysanthemums and roses. There were a few other flowers, but Lily hadn't a clue as to what they were called. Lily was a born-and-bred townie, flowers didn't enter into the equation; she'd never received a bunch of flowers in her life. Her memory suddenly tweaked as she remembered Chris bringing her a massive bunch of bluebells when she had Greg and some wild dog roses when she had Jess. She really was a sweet kid, and no mistaking. Babs was another matter. Babs was all for one and one for all!

Approaching the back door, Alf turned to her with a cheeky grin. 'If this was the front door, Lily, I might be inclined to pick you up and carry you across the threshold. We never did that when we married, did we?'

To her amazement, she found she was blushing again; she gave him a push, saying, 'Open the door, will you, Alf Brown? I ain't got all bloody day, you know.' Whatever he was up to, she thought she'd better watch her step from now on. After all, he might literally be leading her up the garden path.

She gasped aloud at the size of the kitchen. 'My God, this room is bigger than all the houses I've ever lived in. It's beautiful, Alf, and it's really yours, not rented, you're buying it?'

'I own it.'

'This is unreal,' she muttered, drinking it all in as she walked around, noting all the cupboards and longing to look inside, but thinking she hadn't better be nosy. A double-drainer sink caught her eye. She saw there was a washing machine and refrigerator installed in a separate room.

'There's no two ways about it, this house is blooming posh,' she declared, looking around admiringly.

'Go on, Lily, have a look at anything you want. I know you're dying to have a good old nose.' He urged her on, opening cupboards at random, pointing out sets of matching china such as she'd never seen in her life. Canteens of silver cutlery greeted her awestruck eyes, polished to a brilliant brightness.

She made her way out of the kitchen into the hall where Alf pointed out the tiled floor. 'It's a Victorian geometric design, I've had it cleaned by a specialist firm and it's come up a treat.'

She nodded, appreciating everything she saw – not that she understood what a Victorian geometric design was, but she thought it best to acknowledge him. There was even a beautiful stained-glass window in the front hall.

Closed doors lining the hallway asked invitingly to be opened. To her delight Alf opened each one, and again she was astounded at the size and the luxurious furnishings in all of the rooms. There was a breakfast room, parlour, dining room, a lounge with a crystal chandelier at either end, and at the end of the hall was a small comfortably furnished room. She tried to store everything she saw in her memory to tell the girls when she returned home.

Taking her arm, he escorted her up an elegant staircase and, walking beside her along the corridor, he opened a door. Inside was a bedroom with a huge double bed. There were many beautiful features in the room; she gasped aloud with delight. Alf opened a door on the far side of the room and showed her a small dressing room. Another door opened into a bathroom and the facing door linked to another large bedroom. She knew without him telling her the bedroom was his, and the thought chased through her mind that he had another woman. She was surprised at the bolt of jealousy snaking through her.

Continuing the tour up to the second floor, he asked her if she liked the house.

'What a daft question, Alf Brown. Of course I do; it's bloody gorgeous. Only a mug would dislike it.'

He had to laugh, Lily never pulled her punches.

The Other Place

Pointing up a narrow wooden staircase, he informed her that was where the servants' bedrooms used to be. 'Maybe I'll show you another time.'

She quirked an eyebrow. 'Another time?'

Taking her arm, he led her back down the main staircase into the small furnished room on the ground floor.

'Sit down, Lily. There's something I want to ask you.' Wagging a finger at her when she went to say something, he added, 'Please, don't interrupt.'

Hands folded in her lap, she watched him as he paced the small room. 'Come on, Alf, it's not like you to be so reticent.'

'All right, Lily. I want you and the kids back in my life.'

Seeing her ready to say something, he held up his hand to stop her.

'I know I was a real pig to leave you, and I've regretted it every day since. I should have stayed and talked it over with you. I decided the only thing I could do was to work hard and try to make a lot of money. If I did, then I'd come back for you and the kids with something to show you for all my efforts. I want to give you all a good life from now on. You'll never want for anything ever again. I love you, Lily.'

So saying, he picked up two envelopes from a side table. 'By the way, this would be your room if you decide to come back. You can furnish it just how you want. In fact, you can do all the rooms how you want to, but this will be your own private space.' Passing her the envelopes, she took them

The Other Place

and opened one, removing a huge wad of money.

'Whatever is this for, Alf?' she queried in a shocked voice.

'Buy what you need for the house and yourself and the kids, there's plenty more where that came from if you need it.' He smiled at her benevolently.

Opening the second envelope, Lily was stunned after reading Alf had left everything he owned to her in his will.

'You can take it to any solicitor you like in Birmingham and get it checked out,' he told her, running his hands worriedly through his hair; it was obvious he was trying to convince her of his best intentions.

'What's the catch, Alf?' she asked in her forthright manner.

'There's no catch. I want to share the house and everything with you and the kids.'

'Kids? Does that include Babs and Chrissie?'

For a split-second she could have sworn he hesitated. 'Of course it does.'

'Take me home at once, Alf, I have some thinking to do.'

He looked flabbergasted. 'You mean you've got to think about it?'

'Of course, I'll have to discuss it with the family first. I can't just spring something like this on them.' Her mind was already made up, but it wouldn't do to let him know straight away.

'There's more to show you, Lily. Shall I pick you up tomorrow?' he asked as he pulled up outside her house a short while later.

Shaking her head, she jumped out of the car

The Other Place

telling him to come round in a couple of days and she'd give him her decision. Her fingers were crossed behind her back as she told him.

'Please, Lily,' he wheedled.

'No, Alf, I've just told you, come back in a couple of days. I never wanted wealth; you know I married you for love.' Slamming the door hard, she headed across the green, noting the curtains twitching as the neighbours watched her.

***

Alf winced as he drove off, hoping against hope that Lily and the kids would soon come back to him. He had missed them every day since leaving. He was longing to see Jessica and Greg. Not Chrissie, though. No way did he want her anywhere near him, she was too fey for him, and anyway, he wasn't her dad. He'd put up with her if he had to and hope she would soon marry, and that would be that as far as he was concerned. Thank goodness the other one was married now and out of the way. Recalling all the things Chrissie used to say made him grimace in distaste; other disturbing memories returned, but he closed his mind to those. She was daft, no doubt about it, she was never right in the head.

'Why,' he asked himself, 'should they enjoy any of my wealth?' Just the thought of having them under his roof made his blood boil and he longed to stick his foot down hard on the accelerator and burn the miles up in the shortest time possible. Seeing them constantly reminded him of Lily's first marriage. Their presence in his life drove him insane. He would like them to disappear completely from his life; only then would he feel content with his own small family.

***

'But Chris, I've got to think of Jessica and Gregory,' Lily argued.

'I'm not telling you not to go. What I'm saying is, I won't go with you,' she remonstrated, pushing her hair back from her eyes. For once, Chrissie had found the strength of character to stand up for herself. She was determined to keep as far away from Alf Brown as possible. She suspected he had something to do with the trauma she had suffered from for so long.

'What do you mean, you won't come with us? You'll have everything in the world that you'd ever want or dreamed of.'

'You'll never understand, Mom, will you? I don't want to live with him. I'm going to be blunt – I hate him, always have, and so has Babs. I'll find somewhere else to live. You go with the two youngsters. I'll be fine. I've a good idea where I can stay until I sort a flat out.'

'I'm not happy about this, Chris, but I can't turn him down or I think he'll go to the courts to get the kids off me. He can offer them everything money can buy. He'll have them and I'll never get to see them again.'

'I know, Mom, but you've always told us money isn't everything. Love counts for more.' Here was

The Other Place

further proof that Alf Brown came before her.

She jumped up, fetched her coat and told her mom, 'I'll see you later.' She ran straight to Kitty's house.

***

'All sorted,' she announced cheerily later that night. 'I've a room I can move into whenever I want to go.' She held out her hand showing a shiny front-door key.

'You don't hang around, girl, do you? Where is this place? I ain't said you can move out yet.'

'Mom, it's at a woman called Kitty's house. She's a nice person. I've known her a while. And I am twenty-one, you know.' She laughed.

'You're still my responsibility, while you're living at home. How did you get to know this woman?'

'She's helping me with... erm... things. Want a cuppa?'

'Don't change the subject. I ain't daft. I bet it's about them there funny things, I remember you telling me about them. I bet this woman is one of them there spiritualist people.' Seeing her daughter's guilty face, she continued. 'I'm right, you've been mixing with her, and she's one of them. You have, ain't you?'

'Mom, she's helped me a lot, really she has.'

'I suppose that's something, but I don't like your deceit, my girl.' Lily was slightly mollified; she'd been worried about Chrissie's strange talk and often wondered how Alf had managed to stop her

The Other Place

daughter mentioning it. Trouble was, sometimes she'd heard her cry out in the night. She was more concerned at what the neighbours would think more than anything.

'I wasn't being deceitful. Oh, Mom, please don't let's fall out. I'll go and make us a cuppa.'

Putting her sewing down, Lily hoped she'd never have to patch another ripped sheet ever again after she moved in with Alf. *After all, if he's rich,* she mused, *I'll buy everything new instead of mending the old ones.*

She wanted to see him again. His wealthy lifestyle beckoned, and secretly she was looking forward to her new way of life, but knew she would miss her neighbours and her home. She was also concerned about her daughter, but on reflection Chris was twenty-one and quite old enough to look after herself.

Bab's reaction when she had heard the news earlier was unrepeatable, but she wished her mother well and asked, albeit a trifle sarcastically, if she'd be allowed to visit her.

'There'd be more than trouble if he refuses, I can tell you,' Lily retorted. 'You're our daughter, whether Alf likes it or not. As soon as I'm settled I'll let you know, and you can visit whenever you want. I'm your mom, you daft woman, of course you can come round and see us. We're your family. I haven't told your Gran yet. I dunno what she'll say. I think I'll wait until I've moved and tell her when it's all done and dusted. Your aunts and uncles will be more than surprised at my good luck. I expect they'll put themselves out to visit me now

I'll be living somewhere posh. Well, they needn't bother themselves.'

Babs smiled. Lily was getting into her stride and before she went any further, she had her own news to tell.

'Ma, I'm pregnant,' she said interrupting her flow.

'Heh? You what, you daft mare? How could you be so bloody stupid?' Grabbing her daughter in a hug, a frisson of fear shot through Lily. She saw trouble ahead for Babs. 'What's Alan say?'

'I haven't told him yet. I only had it confirmed today and thought I'd tell you first. Don't worry, Mom, Alan will love his son or daughter as soon as it arrives.'

Lily sat, head in hands; how could her daughter be so blind? She was intelligent and had an excellent job, now look at her, living in a tied flat in Kings Heath. How were they ever going to be able to afford to buy a house? A thought entered her head: of course, once she was established in Alf's house, she'd be able to help her two eldest daughters out in more ways than one.

'Alan's going to love it, whether it's a boy or a girl,' Babs declared mutinously.

'Yes, well, you get along home. I've got to see to the kids and do my hair.'

'So, you're dolling yourself up for Alf after the way he treated you?' She could have bitten her tongue out at her words. She loved her mom and would never want to hurt her. 'Sorry, Mom, I'll go. I hope it goes all right for you when you see him again,' she said, trying to make amends.

The Other Place

Babs still detested Alf as much as ever. She knew her mom loved him and the two younger kids more than her and Chris. She had often said to her sister, 'It stands to reason; she hates our real-father. No doubt we remind her of him every time she looks at us and 'er don't wanna keep seeing him. Wasn't our fault though, was it, Chrissie? We d'ain't asked to be born, did we?' Her speech tended to revert to slang when she got stressed.

'I've got to do me hair ready for work. I ain't seeing Alf until the day after tomorrow, for your information, madam,' Lily remarked. *Yes, I will doll myself up for him, and it's none of her business or anyone else's. I'm going to do the best for my kids; they deserve it.* Plus, she missed Alf and was longing to be back in his arms, and his bed.

***

'I knew he'd leave you once you told him as you was pregnant.' Lily was furious. 'I warned ya, you silly cow, why did you do it, eh? He said as he didn't want kids, so you go and get yourself pregnant.'

'But Mom, I want a baby, and I thought he would accept it.'

'Well, ya should 'ave listened to me, shouldn't you?' Arms folded, lips clenched tightly together in disapproval, she felt like slapping her daughter and punching Alan. Sighing, she said, 'What ya gonna do now? I don't know if Alf would let you...'

'No way, I'd live on the streets before I'd consider moving in with him. You know full well

The Other Place

my feelings about him. I'll be moving in with Chris and Kitty. At least I'll be welcome there.'

Lily looked shamefaced, but was secretly relieved. She didn't want the arguments starting up again between her daughter and husband. She rued the day Babs had married Alan Gray. Still, shrugging her shoulders, Babs had made her bed and had to lie on it, wherever it happened to be.

***

One night, the sisters were sitting by the fire with Kitty.

'You look tired, sis,' Chrissie murmured.

'It's hard work carrying a baby. I never thought I'd get this exhausted,' she said drowsily. 'I'll probably have an early night.'

Chrissie yawned in sympathy. 'I'm worn out as well,' she murmured. As she gazed into the fire, pictures began to form of another time and place.

***

'Is that you, Ella?'

Ella swung around at the sound of her name being called.

'Hello, Amy.' She smiled in pleasure at seeing her friend running towards her, her dark blue cloak and dress sweeping the floor as she hurried towards her. Ella had met Amy at one of the houses where she did her storytelling. She had been visiting one of her friends at a house where Ella worked. An instant rapport had been struck up when they had

The Other Place

literally bumped into each other as Ella was leaving the nursery after finishing her storytelling for the day. She thought there was something familiar about Amy, as if she had known her before, but she couldn't think where they might have met. Autumn leaves swirled around the young women as they walked along the road.

'It's good to find time to spend together,' Ella said.

'Indeed it is.' Amy's green eyes twinkled with happiness. Ella felt light-hearted at the thought of being in the company of her new friend.

Ella's fame had quickly spread around the wealthy folk of Birmingham, and she had been inundated with requests to visit houses in and around the city to tell her stories to the children of the house. She was building up a good reputation for reliability and was popular with the youngsters. They constantly asked her for one more story before she left. Ella was nearly always invited back to tell more stories.

A few of her clients had got together and a couple of afternoons each week she told stories to groups of children. She never ran out of ideas – as quickly as she told one story, another began to take shape in her mind. She had started to write them down.

Only this morning, one of her ladies had asked her if she could visit a friend's home two mornings a week.

Mentioning this to Amy as they walked towards the city centre, Amy chuckled, digging her friend in the ribs. 'Oh, my goodness, you're going to be

The Other Place

known as the Birmingham Storyteller.'

Ella stopped in her tracks, eyes opening wide. 'Do you think so?'

'Why not? After all, it's what you do.'

'I suppose it is,' she ruminated. 'I never really thought about it.' Suddenly, she felt light-headed and gripped her friend's arm tightly.

'Ella, are you all right? Here, lean against this wall for a second. You look as if you have seen a ghost.'

Her friend shuddered at her words. *If only you knew the truth of it, Amy.* 'I'm fine, really I am, it's just a sudden dizzy spell.' Shaking her head gently, she blinked hard, trying to dispel the images of the group of women she had seen herself talking to in a strangely furnished room. She and the women had been dressed in clothing very different to today's fashion. The women were wearing trousers and white coats, which she found astonishing as she had never seen women dressed in such outfits before. A few had been dressed in skirts, but the skirts were far shorter than those worn at this time. She felt confused by these sightings and wondered what was happening to her.

She had also been having other visions since doing this job, and the trapped feelings she had suffered with for so long, were beginning to manifest again. How she wished she had someone to discuss her problems with. What was happening to her was all very disturbing, and she was afraid, not understanding the reason for it. Looking at Amy, she wondered what she would say if she told her. Would she think she had taken leave of her

The Other Place

senses? Or would she understand and be able to give her advice?

Watching the fleeting emotions chase across her friend's face, Amy wished Ella would share whatever was troubling her. She had noticed on the last few occasions when they had met up, Ella had a worried air about her and had been looking rather peaky and tired. She was getting concerned, particularly after just seeing her friend have a dizzy spell.

Turning to her, she pleaded, 'Can't you tell me what's wrong? I know it would help.'

Ella hesitated. Could she tell her friend about the sightings which she was certain were from another time?

She shook her head. 'It's nothing really, Amy, honestly, it's simply me being silly. I'm fine now. We'd better carry on with our walk into town or it will be time to go back before we've started!'

Walking along the crowded pavements, Ella was glad of Amy's company as she wasn't at all happy when surrounded by groups of people. She disliked being too close to anyone apart from her friend. From the beginning, she had never felt threatened by Amy's presence. True, at times she felt as if she wanted her own space, but she accepted this happened with most people.

Linking arms, they continued their walk. Worried about Ella, Amy suggested they should go into the park they were passing to see if the swans were on the pool. 'It's better we don't go into town today as you're a little under the weather.'

Nodding her assent, the young woman felt a

The Other Place

warm glow spread throughout her body at her friend's words. She moved a little closer to her, enjoying the feeling of closeness. 'I've always wanted to see a black swan.' A distant memory tugged at her.

'Black swans? I've never heard of those. Where did you hear about them?'

'Erm, I don't know, how strange. I can't remember.' As much as she tried, Ella found she drew a blank trying to recall where she had heard about black swans. 'It's so strange, Amy, it seems to have slipped my memory.' Worry creased her brow.

***

Together, they walked around the park watching the children playing chase and catch the ball. Nursemaids were pushing prams with their charges warmly wrapped up against the cold. There were dogs leaping and running around; Ella sighed at the normality of the scene. *Thank goodness for Amy*, she sighed happily, *where would I be without her?*

That night, Ella dreamt she was walking around a large pool surrounded by tall pine trees; behind the trees was a building she had never seen before. As she strolled around the pool, strangers greeted her cheerily. 'Nice day, luv, out for a walk, are you?'

She felt herself nodding and smiling in return as she happily surveyed the scene. Suddenly, to her amazement as she glanced down, she saw she was wearing a skirt that showed her legs. Horrors! What would people think? Her eyes cautiously climbed up her legs; up and up, it seemed never-ending when she came to the hem of the shortest skirt she

The Other Place

had ever worn in her life. Hands tugging, she tried pulling the offending garment down to cover her modesty. She suddenly stopped, realising if she pulled too hard, she would probably pull it off. Her face went bright red with embarrassment, and glancing surreptitiously around, she was more than shocked to see other women and young girls in similar attire. Wondering if they were all dressed for a fancy dress outing, she moved quickly to a nearby bench. Sitting felt very uncomfortable. Aware that someone had sat beside her, she turned her head.

'Amy, where on earth did you spring from?' she laughed.

'I'm always around for you, you know I am!'

Her eye caught a sudden movement on the pool and a collective gasp filled the air as a flock of black swans glided gracefully across the water, barely causing a ripple to spread across the pool's surface. Ella forgot everything as she concentrated on the beauty of the scene before her eyes. The scene gradually faded away as she slid deeper into sleep.

CHAPTER 9

Lily was fed up. She liked her new home, but found she didn't have enough to do to occupy her mind; most of the time she was bored almost to tears. Time hung heavily on her hands. Boredom caught her trailing her fingers along shelves and sideboards to see if the daily help had missed a speck of dust. She wouldn't have said anything to the daily help if she had found any; she would have simply fetched a duster and cleaned it herself. Lily used to love cleaning. She derived a great deal of satisfaction in polishing windows and furniture and floors. Mind you, this house was a hundred times larger than anywhere she had ever lived before so she obviously needed help. Having always been a busy person, she couldn't adjust to this enforced idleness.

A memory of fetching the sheets in from the clothes line in the wintertime flashed through her mind. The sheets had been stiff as boards. She giggled to herself at the memory, wondering how she'd never tripped over them as she had struggled into the house with her arms full. She'd been so cold it was a wonder she had never had chilblains on her fingers.

Babs and Chrissie had had chilblains on their toes when they were young due to the holes in their shoes; they used cardboard to try and keep the wet out, but that would get soggy. 'Poor kids,' she murmured, remembering the state their feet had got into – she'd used calamine lotion on them to stop the itching. Greg and Jess will never suffer like that, not now they were a million times better off. *Or are we?* Maybe financially, but did she really enjoy this lifestyle or was she missing the comradeship she had always had with her friends and neighbours? She certainly didn't miss the flat irons, having to spit on them to make sure they were hot enough to do the ironing; had always turned her stomach inside out.

Lily regretted that she was not closer to her older daughters, but what could she do? She had to put the younger ones first, they were Alf's children.

If only our Chris hadn't been so strange. Her having an imaginary friend upset Alf; why, she never understood. Lots of kids had make-believe friends. She'd try to tell him but he would fly into one of his rages, and threaten to belt Chrissie one and lock her in the cupboard again. She shuddered with guilt at the horror this must have caused her daughter. Still, it was Chris's fault wasn't it? If she hadn't acted so daft Alf wouldn't have done it in the first place.

Realising she didn't have enough to occupy her thoughts during the daytime, she determined to find a new hobby or she would go mad; suddenly, it came to her.

I'll learn to drive. Once I've passed my test, it will make life so much easier for me. Excitedly, she looked through the advertisements in the telephone directory for driving instructors in her area. Finding one, she rang the number and made an appointment. She knew Alf would buy her a new car and her imagination took flight. *I'll be able to visit the girls and go shopping in town; maybe I'll get closer to them. I can apologise to Chrissie for what Alf did to her. Try to build bridges.*

***

Tripping down the steps to the waiting car, Lily was startled to see how good-looking her driving instructor was. He was smiling and holding the car door open for her. He was younger than her. Tall, dark and ruggedly handsome would have been her description if anyone had asked her. He was also very smartly dressed; this was something Lily admired in a man. Top of her list as far as men were concerned were good manners and well dressed. *So how come I married Alf?* she would ask herself from time to time.

Settling herself comfortably onto the cool leather of the driving seat, she listened nervously as the instructor proceeded to give her a list of instructions. She listened carefully as she wanted to pass her test in record time.

Her instructor's voice set her nerves jangling, she found it so sexy. This was an unknown happening for Lily. Other men had never made any impression on her before. After Alf had left her, she'd had offers to go out from different men, but had always refused. If any man gave her the come-on, he was very quickly slapped down. Now here she was sitting in the close confines of a stranger's car, and his sexy voice was distracting her from

The Other Place

hearing his instructions.

'Concentrate, Lily,' his voice rasped. She jumped – how she admired a strong, dominant man. Her heart skipped a beat, and she wondered how on earth she was going to learn to drive with such a distraction.

'Hand on the gear stick,' he said, his large suntanned hand covering her small hand. This was getting too much for her, and she shifted uncomfortably in her seat. His hand felt so right covering hers. It was warm, and she was sure she could feel his pulse beating through her skin. Tingles ran up her arm, her heart was leaping about in her chest, and she felt a flush rising from her neck to her cheeks. My goodness, she was reacting like a teenager.

'Call me Pete,' he told her huskily, proceeding to inform her about the controls, leaving his hand over hers on the gear stick. She was finding it extremely difficult to concentrate and found she was mesmerised for the whole hour of the lesson. Nothing this exciting had ever happened to her before. Some of the instructions had obviously sunk in as she had managed a short drive around the local streets.

Dropping her back at her house, he gave her what she thought was the sexiest grin she had ever seen, as he asked, 'Do you want to book another lesson, Lily?' Did she ever? She thought she would like to sit beside him all day, every day, smelling his wonderful aftershave and feeling the heat of his body emanating across the car.

Trying to appear calm and serene, she asked if

he had another slot free during the week. He booked her in for Friday.

Floating back into the house, her mind was buzzing with the lesson and the vibes she had picked up from Pete.

***

Peter, meanwhile, drove away knowing he had made another conquest. *And what a little stunner this one is,* he thought, chuckling, busily planning how to get her back to his flat. Pete loved the ladies.

***

'I had me first driving lesson today, Alf,' she told him excitedly whilst having tea.

He pulled a face. 'Sure you can trust him, Lil?' He was slurping his tea much to her disgust.

She'd never noticed he had that nasty habit before.

'Course I can. He was very good.' *Extremely good,* she thought dreamily, remembering the touch of his hand as she changed gear. She closed her mind to thoughts of how his hand would feel elsewhere on her body.

'Lily, you never answered me.'

'Sorry, Alf, what did you say?'

'You thinking of your driving instructor?' he asked jealously.

'Course not. You are a silly old fool.' She jumped up and walked around the table. Standing behind him, she dropped butterfly kisses on his hair and down his neck.

'Stop it, or I'll be forced to take you to bed,' he groaned.

'Come on, then,' she urged, taking his hand and pulling him up. 'How about we do it in front of the fire in the lounge?'

'Yes.' Wrapping his arms around her slender body, he kissed her deeply, sending her senses reeling. 'Oh, Alf, hurry up. I can't wait.' What did she need a driving instructor for when she had the real thing right here?

***

Lily's driving lessons had been progressing well. The sexual spark was alive between her and Pete, but she had deliberately kept it at that: just a spark. No way was she going to let it ignite. Alf was her man, she told herself firmly – one man, one woman. The trouble was she fancied Pete something rotten. She often found herself wondering what it would be like to go to bed with him, but she knew she never would. Alf satisfied her every need and as much as she desired Pete, she wouldn't be able to live with her guilt if she cheated on her husband.

Driving fascinated her and she decided that when she had passed her test, she would do a basic course in mechanics. Life was suddenly more interesting and instead of feeling tired and discontented, not wanting to get up in the morning, she looked forward to every day; her weekdays were full of new and exciting ideas.

The Other Place

She had something different to do every day.

Monday afternoon was when she took her first driving lesson of the week. She had her hair done in preparation in the morning. She had to look good for Pete to keep the spark going, she told herself. Seeing Pete added a frisson of excitement to the start of her week, and she really looked forward to her lesson. There was definitely something attractive about him, not just sexual, either – although she enjoyed the feeling he engendered in her, she also liked talking to him and thought he would make a good friend. Lily hoped that once she had passed her driving test she wouldn't lose contact with him.

Tuesdays, she had taken up art and discovered she had a real gift.

Wednesday was a brilliant day for Lily; secretly she had always been fond of the sound of the Celtic Harp, she had first heard it on the radio and fallen in love with the sound. With Alf being so rich, she had no hesitation in treating herself to one. A tutor came to the house to give her instructions.

Thursdays, she had her hair restyled and a facial… after all, she had to look good for her driving lesson the following day.

Friday morning was given over to a two-hour driving lesson; she was determined to pass her test first time.

All in all, life was good. She missed her old friendships, but was determined to forge a new life for herself.

One thing clouding her horizon was Alf's attitude to Chrissie and Babs; she could sense he

The Other Place

still resented them, as whenever she mentioned their names he would change the subject. She'd never forgotten how he had called Chris a daftie, his words had gone deep. Try as she might to explain her middle daughter's *dreams*, as she called them, nothing would alter his view.

Lily had to admit Chris was different, but she wasn't daft, far from it. *Perhaps*, she thought ruefully, *if I had listened to her more when she was a babby, it would have helped.* She recalled when Chris was a toddler how she would chatter on and on for hours, laughing and giggling and pointing to things, as if she was speaking to someone.

Guilt smote her as she recalled all the times she'd pushed her daughter away when she'd tried telling her about her friends. She was now certain she really could see these people. *To think I even smacked her one across the face at times. No wonder she never spoke to me about it again, I even told her to shut up in the kitchen at Fellfeld when she was trying to tell me about it. Poor kid.*

Perhaps if I'd taken notice in the first place, she wouldn't have started screaming and shouting out in her sleep, obviously terrified of something. Even then I didn't go to her because Alf told me he'd give her a good hiding.

She decided to buy Chrissie something nice in the hope it would help make amends. It would never enter Lily's head to think of discussing anything about what had happened in the past with her daughter. It was all too strange by far.

Anyway, she thought, brushing her new grey suit down, *my daughter could have landed up in the lunatic asylum if Alf hadn't shut her in the cupboard, then what*

The Other Place

would the neighbours have said?

***

Peter was puzzled. Despite his best efforts, he was getting nowhere fast with Lily. The chemistry was well and truly alive between them, but he couldn't get beyond the initial spark. This was making him desire her more, and he found himself fantasying about her at times when he should be concentrating on his other pupils. There was no doubt about it, she had really got under his skin.

Sitting beside her in the car, he wanted nothing more than to reach out and kiss her. *Stop it,* he told himself, *and concentrate on your work.* He couldn't understand why he should be more attracted to her than any other of his pupils. Admittedly, the other women he'd had affairs with had been easy prey; they had fallen willingly into his waiting arms. Lily was different. She was a little older than his usual women friends; this didn't worry him as there was something very alluring about her. He couldn't say what it was exactly, but he simply had to have her, and the more she resisted his advances, the more he wanted her.

She was doing extremely well with her lessons. Her test would be here soon, and he was desperate to get her back to his flat and into bed. Last Saturday he had bought a bottle of champagne for when she finally succumbed to his charms; he was convinced she would. The thought of going to bed with her made him break into a sweat. Thinking of her lying naked next to him made his pulse race.

The Other Place

Gosh, she was a little stunner; he really would like to get to know her better. Despite her chatter, she never gave much away. He knew she was married, but nothing else. He would go over their conversations at night when he sat in his bachelor flat, complete with its double bed, trying to see if she'd given even a hint of fancying him, but so far he didn't seem to have gained many points. But the attraction was there, it surrounded them in the confines of the car, and it was driving him insane.

When Pete had first met Lily, he thought she would be a nice little dalliance. There was certainly a spark between them, but for some reason or other it had gone no further. Lily had backed away. True, she still flirted with him, batting her eyelashes and casting him sexy glances, and occasionally giving him a quick flash of her thigh when she settled into her seat. He knew all the tricks that women deployed when they fancied a bloke. Now he was getting seriously worried he was losing his charm or charisma, whatever you called it. The more she resisted him, the more he wanted her.

Why did Lily attract him? Was it because she was such a happy little soul, or maybe it was simply because she refused to take the relationship one step further. Maybe his pride was wounded. He couldn't wait for Mondays and Fridays when her driving lesson was due. The thought of her sent his senses reeling and he could never work out how he kept his hands to himself during the lesson.

Whenever he thought of her he smiled.

***

The Other Place

Lily was looking forward to her driving lesson this Monday. Admiring herself in the full-length mirror, she considered she looked pretty good for her age.

She wasn't very tall, admittedly, but everything was in proportion. In fact, she was a bit on the small side, but Alf loved her and to her nothing else mattered, really. She would have liked her breasts to be a little larger, but there were always falsies if you were lacking in that department and needed a bit of padding out. Actually, she'd never worn them because Alf liked her just the way she was. She smiled thinking of Alf. He'd certainly looked after her since she'd moved back in with him. He'd showered her with the good things in life, and she was grateful. Mind you, lately she had noticed a slackening off on the sexual front, but then her husband was a busy man, and he was getting older. She missed his attentions, but thought when he'd sorted his business matters out, they'd be back to normal. She was missing the sex.

The thing was, his business seemed to have taken over his life in recent weeks and it was all he could think and talk about. At times, Lily thought the business had become his mistress and she was jealous of the hours he devoted to it. She seethed with rage when he sat in his chair with a distant look in his eyes. Knowing he wasn't thinking about her turned her stomach upside down and she found herself thinking of Pete on these occasions. At these times, she would remember her time at Fellfeld and wonder if she had been happier then;

after all, she could never remember being bored. She dismissed Fellfeld – it was in the past – and began counting the positives of what she now had.

Smoothing her blouse over her bust, she thought wickedly, *I'll flirt with Pete, but that's as far as it will go. I just want a bit of fun. Alf's so worried about work, he's not paying me any attention.* Lily needed constant reassurance to keep her confidence up.

Hitching her skirt up higher, she got into the driver's seat. Pete shifted uncomfortably in his seat and she smiled to herself. Knowing she could have him anytime she liked sent a frisson of excitement through her. She told herself to concentrate on her driving otherwise she would cause an accident.

Pete decided to try the professional approach; shutting the exciting vision of her kissing him out, he delivered his instructions in clipped tones. He had to, or his voice would have been shaking!

Lily was bemused. She had sprayed herself with her favourite perfume, the one she knew drove Alf mad with desire, and she had made herself as attractive as possible, but Pete wasn't reacting. After glancing at her, it was as if he had steeled himself against her. She'd deliberately moved herself back in the seat so her skirt would ride up even higher. She saw him glance, but he quickly looked away. She was rattled; after all, she'd taken great pains today. Tormenting Pete was a game to her, and she was acutely disappointed he had shown no reaction.

***

The Other Place

'Friday?' he queried, pen posed over his diary, desperately trying not to look at her; if he did he would be lost. *Please let her say yes to Friday or I'll never survive.*

'Yes, that's fine.' She tried to sound as cool and distant as he had, but there was a small tremor of disappointment in her voice. Her game had failed today, and she couldn't understand why. Perhaps he had found someone new. Oh no, she hoped he hadn't, she looked forward to flirting with him; it helped the rejected feeling she was suffering from with Alf being so busy. She would try and dream up something new for Friday.

Giving him a flirty smile, she jumped out of the car letting him see just enough thigh and cleavage for decency's sake.

Three days to go before she saw Pete again. *I have to have a plan,* she deliberated, *he can't go off me yet.* Going through her wardrobe, she suddenly realised what she was doing and started to laugh. *Acting like a teenager at my age,* she berated herself, *just grow up, Lily Brown.*

Chapter 10

Babs rocked her son to sleep in the flat she shared with Chrissie in Kings Heath. It had become a bit crowded at Kitty's house, but glancing around this new place, Babs sulkily thought, *This ain't much better, but it's a bit of a start, and we ain't getting in Kitty's way.* Even Babs with all her self-centred ways could see the older woman was ill.

She was besotted with Simon. Just three months old, he was the most beautiful baby in the whole wide world, as she was fond of telling all and sundry. She missed Alan, but there was no way she would give up Simon for him; he was her world and Alan could get on with his own life.

She felt quite bitter at times, a new emotion for her after she had loved Alan for what seemed like her whole life. Not that she was that old, but he was the only man she had ever known. The sex had never really appealed to her very much, it had hurt her, but she had put up with it as she was so desperate for a baby. *If only I could talk to our Chris about it, but she's so fey she'd never understand what I'm on about.*

Chrissie, for some reason or other, had never to her knowledge had a boy-friend, so there was no point in trying to talk to her. When out of sheer desperation she had tried, her sister would skilfully change the subject, fast. Apart from which, she didn't want to add to her sister's worries; some nights, she heard her shouting and screaming out in her sleep. Babs would have liked a chat about relationships and particularly marriage, but she had no married friends; in fact, like her sister, she had very few friends. Sylvia, her best friend, had left the area in pursuit of her celebrity career.

'You not got a boyfriend yet then, Chris?'

Her sister blushed scarlet.

'Blimey, I was only asking if you had a boyfriend, that's all. It's not like I was asking for personal details!'

'I'm far too busy to think about relationships. How do you feel about going to the pictures with me one Saturday night for a change? Do us good to go to the Gaumont up town, they're showing *Breakfast at Tiffany's*, I'd love to see it. Or we could go to the Kingsway, what do you think?'

'I dunno. Simon's a bit young to be left. We'll ask Mom tomorrow, see what she says. I know Alf won't let her look after him, but she might know someone we could trust.' Babs had to smile at how adroitly her sibling managed to change the subject whenever she mentioned men.

Relieved at managing to change the conversation, Chrissie offered to do her hair.

'Be nice if we had a small radio, wouldn't it?' Babs said, as her sister back-combed her hair.

'Mmm, there are some smashing songs out by The Supremes, and Cliff Richard and the Shadows.'

'Yes, they're okay, Chris, but I still love Elvis, he's The King, Mom likes him as well. I'm going to have a posh radio, a television and a Dansette record player when I have my own place. I'm gonna have everything.'

Later, lying in bed, Babs thought, despite all her plans, life looked very bleak. After all, what man would ever want to take her out? She had a young child and a husband somewhere or other. She had heard Alan had moved abroad to work. He had sent her money for a while, but since she'd moved house the money had dried up. 'Mean pig,' she would chunter under her breath whenever she thought about it. She'd sent her new address to his home, so he had no excuse.

CHAPTER 11

Amy hurried along the streets, holding her skirt high above the filthy pavements. There were a few dog walkers out and about. It was a Sunday morning and she was on her way to Ella's flat. Men and young boys were out shovelling up the horse dung and the debris from the previous day.

Ella was treating her to lunch and, most exciting of all, she was going to teach Amy how to read the tarot cards and the crystal ball. She knew her parents would disapprove of this new venture, but to learn how to predict the future fascinated her and she couldn't wait to start the first lesson.

Ella had come across some old tarot cards and a crystal ball in a second-hand shop in Birmingham. She had been delighted at her ability to be able to read the cards and the crystal almost immediately. She was looking forward to showing Amy how to interpret them as she was certain her friend would be an excellent pupil.

'My, you're early,' Ella greeted her, letting her into the flat. 'I'm still in my dressing gown!'

'I know, but I'm so keen to learn. You don't mind, do you?' A winsome smile crossed her features, and Ella shook her head. Her hair was hanging loose, and Amy put out her hand and gently ran her fingers through it.

'You have beautiful hair,' she murmured, kissing her cheek, and then as if she was overcome

The Other Place

with emotion, she drew her friend into a tight hug.

'Oh, thank you.' Ella wasn't sure what to say or how to react to another woman kissing and hugging her.

'Leave your jacket here,' she said, pointing to the hangers in the small passageway. 'I'll just fix my hair and get dressed.'

'Don't worry about me,' Amy countered, 'you look so pretty like that.'

Ella's eyes opened wide in surprise; in all her life no one had ever told her she was pretty. Ugly, yes, pretty, never.

'You think I'm pretty?' she stuttered in astonishment, pushing a long strand of hair from her face.

Amy walked across the room and began rearranging Ella's hair.

'There now, you look lovely.' She planted another kiss on her cheek, making her friend blush to the roots of her hair.

'I'll be back shortly, Amy, perhaps you could make some tea, and the biscuit tin is full.'

Never having had a woman friend in her life, Ella wondered if it was normal for women to kiss and hug each other; did all friends act like this? She felt a warm glow spread through her when she remembered Amy had told her she was pretty; she'd quite enjoyed the hug and kiss as well. She worried if this was right, but she couldn't help her feelings, could she? How she adored her new friend.

In her tiny bedroom, she dressed as fast as she could. A prim, white, high-necked cotton blouse and long black skirt covered her practically from head to

The Other Place

foot. She still felt the warmth of Amy's arm around her and remembered the only time she'd ever experienced this before was from her grandmother.

As she got ready, her thoughts turned to the coming lesson, and she was certain her friend was going to enjoy the learning experience. She was enjoying her work and the independence it gave her. Ella missed her grandparents, but realised she couldn't go and see them in case she met her stepfather.

Amy was indeed an apt pupil, and both women were satisfied with the outcome of the first lesson.

'You have a flair for this, Amy, and I know between us we're going to learn even more. I've not been reading the cards or crystal for long so I think we are on an exciting journey of discovery together.'

Later Amy asked her if she would be so kind as to dress her hair into a bun.

Ella willingly agreed. The young women enjoyed experimenting with different hairstyles.

Brushing Amy's long hair, Ella felt her head begin to spin, and she had to sit down quickly. As she combed her friend's hair, she experienced a strange feeling of having done this self-same thing in another time and place.

'Chrissie's time,' she gasped.

'Pardon? Did you say "Chrissie's time"?'

Ella was bemused. 'I don't know what made me say that. Please, forgive me. I really don't feel myself lately.' She took a deep breath.

Amy's hair seemed to shimmer and shine. Her head felt smaller beneath her hands and was now a different shape. She got the impression she was combing a younger person's hair. She was certain it was someone she had known as a friend. She felt overwrought for a moment knowing she was in the future and it was so different to anything she had ever known. She was brushing the long black hair of a young girl, using a flower-backed hairbrush. The room she was in had pictures on the walls signed by someone called Elvis Presley. The girl was singing a song she had never heard before. Glancing down, she saw she was wearing a pretty navy-blue spotted skirt and a pink top. Ella was amazed to find herself in such a situation and was about to gasp aloud when she found herself back in Amy's flat.

'Dearest, whatever is it?' Amy took her friend's hands within hers and gently massaged her wrists. 'Ella, this is the second time this has happened, whatever is wrong with you? Do you need to see a doctor? I'll come with you if you're worried about going.'

Ella knew it wasn't a doctor she needed to see. In fact, a doctor was the last person she wanted to visit. No way could she confide in him. She couldn't understand what was happening to her. She was more than convinced a doctor would send her to the mental hospital. She'd heard bad things about the hospital and avoided it all costs.

'I'll be fine, truly I will. It's just something that happens to me from time to time.'

Amy hugged Ella. 'You can tell me anything, you know, I won't repeat it to anyone.'

The closeness of her friend was so comforting,

The Other Place

Ella wanted to stay within the warmth of her embrace. She felt safe, secure, something she had never really experienced in her life. Snuggling closer she whispered, 'Thank you, dearest Amy, perhaps one day I'll be able to tell you about my life, but not today.'

Reluctantly leaving her friend's arms, she smiled.

'You have a beautiful smile.' Amy stroked her face gently, and then to Ella's amazement she wrapped her arms around her and kissed her on the lips.

Ella shuddered, shocked, realising she had responded to Amy's kiss. It was the first sexual response she had experienced. Drawing back she looked into Amy's green eyes; eyes that mirrored hers.

'Amy, surely women don't kiss each other, surely it's wrong?'

Her friend laughed, 'What's wrong about it? Love knows no boundaries, Ella. It's all about trust, whatever you tell me will go no further.'

As much as Ella loved her friend she decided, no, she would keep everything to herself. It was the safest way. No way could she tell anyone, let alone Ella, about her visions or they would think she was stupid.

A similar thing had occurred a few days ago when she had felt dizzy and found herself once again in another time. There had been people rushing around, going in and out of shops; the buildings were similar to the ones in Birmingham, but different to anything she had seen before.

The Other Place

Everything looked out of focus, as if she was seeing the scenes through misty glass. The people were wearing strange clothes and there were no horse and carriages. Instead, there were extraordinary looking vehicles travelling along the road.

Recalling her earlier dream of the black swans and other incidents, she realised she had somehow visited the future. It was all very puzzling and worrying, but she told herself she had to accept whatever it was happening to her, she couldn't share it with anyone.

***

It was growing dark and Ella lit the candles. They cast shadows into the darkest corners of the room and she felt quite nervous, but constantly reassured herself nothing bad could happen to her. After all, what her stepfather had done was the worst thing ever so what did she have to worry about anyway?

Hearing a sound, she glanced around the room. She shuddered as the fire suddenly flickered brightly sending a shower of sparks into the hearth. 'Hello Amy,' she called out, thinking her friend might be in the hallway.

Despite the warmth of the fire she shuddered again, the room was beginning to feel icy cold. *If only Amy were here.* In her mind she asked if there was anybody there.

'Look into the fire, Ella,' a woman's deep melodious voice ordered her. She looked into the flames spurting up the chimney. 'Start counting backwards from ten,' the voice

instructed her. There was something hypnotic about the deep voice and Ella followed the instructions word for word.

Her head began to spin and darkness descended. The scene before her eyes horrified her. She saw a man dressed in strange clothing dragging a small child by the hand. She heard him saying, 'This'll teach you to say yampy things, my girl. Talking about a friend you haven't got and no one's ever seen, well, this'll stop all of your claptrap. Alf Brown stands no nonsense from idiots like you.' Opening a small cupboard door, he promptly pushed the little girl inside.

'Dare to tell your mother or anyone else about this and you'll know about it,' he told her savagely. Locking the door, he laughed cruelly as he pocketed the key. 'The kid's completely bonkers talking about seeing someone who ain't there. She'll have all the neighbours thinking we're as daft as her. A spell in the cupboard will soon sort her out.'

He laughed again, and grabbing his jacket and cap, he turned around and seemed to stare straight into Ella's eyes. 'You say a word, girl,' he sneered, pointing a dirty finger at her, 'and you'll be for it too.' He slammed the door loudly and somehow she knew he would be on his way out to the local pub.

The awful and frightening thing to Ella was, apart from the fact he could see through time, the man was identical in looks to her stepfather.

Suddenly, she was back in her flat, shaking with horror and fear at what she had just witnessed. The poor child, how could anyone be so cruel to a young child? Remembering how she had felt when she had suffered at the hands of her stepfather, tears sprang to her eyes thinking the youngster might suffer the same feelings of being trapped as she did. *If only I could help her,* she thought.

The Other Place

She was puzzled as to how the man she had just seen could possibly be her stepfather. She was convinced it was him.

Wiping her eyes, Ella replayed the scene in her mind. What a cruel man, but who was he and who was the little girl? How could she help the child? Not understanding why this should have happened, she decided the best place for her to be was bed. At least she could try to relax and get warm.

Lying awake, bad memories flickered at the edge of her consciousness and threatened to prevent the sleep she craved. Over the years she had taught herself to think of positive things rather than concentrate on the negative. Ella had found this helped her enormously, and she began focusing on the good things in her life. The trouble was, the man's face and words kept returning to her; she woke several times in the night. All the bad things that had happened were returning to haunt her. Perhaps it was time to confide in Amy.

***

The following morning, Amy knocked on Ella's front door, she was simply bursting to share some good news with her friend.

Seeing Ella's distraught look, she gasped in shock. 'Whatever is the matter?' Stepping into the hallway, she hurried her friend into the small living room.

'What's happened? Please tell me.'

Ella quickly related what had happened the previous evening and told her why she had run

The Other Place

away from home and gone to live with her grandparents.

The young woman was astounded at Ella's story.

Nodding her head, she told her friend, 'What a dreadful life you've led, Ella. I'm going to help you as much as I can.' She got up from her chair and hurried to her friend, where she gave her the biggest hug. Ella leant into her warmth, welcoming the love and friendship she gave her.

Seeing her friend's pale face and heavy eyes, she added, 'Ella, you have experienced such awful things in your life, and I know that sharing what's happened to you with me will have helped you.' Stroking her friend's hair, trying to offer comfort in any way she could, Amy stared into Ella's green eyes. She gasped on seeing the hurt deep inside her friend. 'Shall I make you a drink?' Amy offered, knowing Ella needed distracting from her thoughts before she went to work later in the day.

'Thanks for offering, but it might help me to busy myself and get my thoughts together if I make it.' She was reluctant to leave the comfort of Amy's arms but slowly got up and went into the kitchen, wondering what was happening to the safe little world she had managed to create.

After finishing their drinks, Amy suggested they went for a walk.

'Come on, time away from the flat will be beneficial to you. Don't forget you have a story time to attend later.' Amy's brisk voice broke Ella's reverie, and she jumped; she had forgotten her appointment. Last night's events had put everything

The Other Place

else out of her mind.

'Good job you reminded me, I'm so tired and confused, I'm having a job thinking straight.'

Strolling along the street, the late autumn sun slanted across the pavements, making the wet leaves shimmer gold and red. Amy held Ella's gloved hand. 'I've been thinking about what you told me, and I know you will probably disagree.' Seeing how sad her friend was, she knew she desperately needed her help.

'I have to make the spirit appear.'

'No!' Ella gasped in panic. 'We don't know what we will unleash.' Tears slid down her pale cheeks which she wiped away with the back of her glove; she allowed her friend to guide her into the small park at the end of the road.

'Amy, no, I won't hear of it,' she said, 'seeing the man from another time was the most terrifying experience of my life.'

'I know you won't believe me, but I understand these matters more than you realise. I want to help you.'

Collapsing onto a nearby bench, Ella gasped in shock at the cold dampness of the seat.

Wrapping her coat more tightly around her against the chilly wind, she drew closer to her friend. 'How will it help me?'

'Because, by facing up to him, he will know he can't threaten you ever again. He has obviously repeatedly used his tactics throughout different lifetimes to threaten and abuse children. By confronting him, you will rid yourself of him, and I feel certain the young girl will find her way through her problems.'

'How do you know these things?'

'I think the spirit world helps me, Ella.'

'You really do believe in spiritual matters?' Turning to face her, 'You also believe in reincarnation as well, don't you?'

'Yes, and you have given me further proof today,'

Ella shook her head, finding the day's revelations a bit too much for her to grasp. 'So the young girl I saw is me in a future lifetime, and somehow it's my bad luck to have the same stepfather again! How unlucky can a girl get?'

'Yes, it is very unfortunate, dear friend.' Patting her knee, she watched as a smartly dressed couple walked their poodle through the park, acknowledging their wave.

'Dearest, there is a reason for you to live through the lifetime. You will have the knowledge and conviction to win through all your difficulties and deal with him once and for all.'

Trembling, Ella asked fearfully, 'Will I see him again in this lifetime?' The thought of ever casting her eyes on him again was abhorrent to her.

'I'm afraid a confrontation is possible.'

Ella was devastated at her words, but grateful for her honesty.

'Amy, about my mother, why did she let him do those dreadful things to me?'

'In this lifetime, she was frightened he would beat her so she let him do whatever he wanted to you. Normally, she was so drunk anyway and hadn't a clue what your evil stepfather was doing.

The Other Place

You should pity your mother because you have escaped, she never will. She will try in the lifetime you saw, but I'm afraid the relationship will not be happy.

Remember, your mother is a simple country woman who has no knowledge of these matters. Any punishment to her is best meted out by the man of the family. To her, when the punishment is over, it's finished; she would never think it could cause lasting damage. She doesn't understand emotional or even physical abuse. Physical damage, yes, the sort you can see, such as a cut, a bruise, or a broken limb, but emotional and physical abuse rarely show, do they? The abusers hit their victims where it's not visible to others.'

Ella acknowledged her words sadly, what she had said made perfect sense. She silently forgave her mother, but secretly hoped she would never have to see her again.

Amy smiled, knowing her friend was taking slow but certain steps on the way to healing.

'There are two things that would prevent your stepfather approaching you again.'

'Tell me quickly what they are,' Ella asked eagerly.

'If he sees you have someone who loves you deeply, he will lose the power to dominate you. At the moment, he knows you aren't in a relationship so he finds it easy to wield his power, and if he sees you are successful he will feel threatened and leave you alone.'

Ella was shocked at her friend's words. 'Oh dear, I have no one who loves me, and doubt if I ever will.'

'You have me and soon enough you will have someone who will love you forever.' Squeezing her friend's hands she asked, 'Where is your story time today?'

'Oh my goodness. It's at the Philpott's. I'd better hurry, I'd forgotten again.'

***

Amy was well aware of her friend's burgeoning interest in Eddie Philpott and vice versa. She knew Eddie quite well and saw him from time to time. Unbeknown to Ella, Eddie often spoke to Amy about the young storyteller, and she knew he would be at the house today. She urged her friend on, knowing she was in for a big surprise.

'Let's walk back to the flat. I think you're feeling a little easier and I don't want you to miss your appointment. We'll call in at the pie shop as we both need lunch. No buts,' she grinned as Ella went to interrupt her, 'you'll feel better for having something substantial inside you.'

As they hurried to the shop, Amy steered her away from the rotting vegetation in the gutter 'Careful, or you'll slip on the foul-smelling mess.'

'Thanks. I wasn't concentrating.'

'I've always been fascinated by the paranormal,' Amy confided as they left the shop. 'My family has no interest and I'm very choosy as to who I speak of such matters with. Not everyone shares this interest.' Stray hairs fell across her eyes and she brushed them aside.

The Other Place

'I'm so pleased you decided to tell me about your terrible experiences, we're true friends now.'

'Are you sure it won't be dangerous trying to raise the spirit?' Ella shuddered again as the bad memory of the previous evening began to resurface, swiftly followed by all the other memories which tormented her.

'No, it's asking for trouble leaving it in abeyance.'

Entering the small living room of Ella's home, they looked around.

'Everything seems all right at the moment,' Amy remarked.

'So there's no need to try to clear the spirit tonight?'

'Yes, there is every need. The spirit may well return at the same time tonight and every following night if we don't face him. He won't return when he realises you are stronger than he is. Now, let's forget about him, we'll eat lunch and then you must get ready for work. I'll walk to the Philpott's with you and come back here tonight.'

Ella was happy to fall in with the arrangements; she didn't know what would have happened to her if Amy hadn't been around. She walked across to her friend and kissed her.

This was out of character for Ella and she felt shocked at her actions; there was something about Amy which fascinated her, and she had to admit she was physically attracted to her. Only her strongly held beliefs stopped her from taking the first step to an affair. She was also scared that should she overstep the mark Amy would break up

The Other Place

their friendship.

Hugging each other, they found themselves enjoying the feeling the closeness brought and held each other for a few minutes longer, each inhaling the scent of the other's body. *If only I had the courage,* Ella thought, *to take the next step.*

Sighing, Amy reluctantly broke away. 'You must hurry, Ella, or you'll be late for work.'

'Oh, yes.' Ella was confused by her feelings, and looking into her friend's eyes she thought she saw her own longings reflected back. Taking a deep breath, she stepped away and busied herself getting ready for work. Her mind was awhirl with the different emotions that Amy had awakened deep within her. Was she wrong to have these feelings about another woman? On reflection she realised it was her need for friendship and comfort that attracted her to Amy.

Amy exuded natural warmth and for a moment Ella had misconstrued her emotions.

***

Ella hadn't seen Eddie Philpott for a while, so she was surprised on entering the nursery to find him standing with his hands clasped behind him and his back to the fire.

She observed once again how tall and elegant he was. His dark hair gleamed in the firelight. Blushing, she removed the thin coat she had acquired from a local second-hand shop. She thought a coat looked far more professional for her type of work than a shawl, but how she missed the

The Other Place

warmth of her shawl.

She was keeping the cloak and bonnet she'd worn for her interview for special occasions. Her grandparents had bought the outfit for her when she had lived with them, she had adored it from the moment she had seen it, and vowed to keep it forever.

Noticing her flushed cheeks, Eddie saw how it enhanced her features and made her even more desirable.

'Victoria and Ralph are finishing their lessons, they won't be long,' he reassured her, noticing her quizzical gaze. 'They always look forward to your stories.'

Smiling at his words, she hung her coat on the peg on the back of the door and then seated herself on one of the dark wooden stools near the fireside.

'Tell me, Miss Earnwell, how you came to be a storyteller.'

Her eyes opened wide at his words. She would never have thought such a good-looking man would be in the least bit interested in talking to her. She was more than a little in love with him, but knew she would never merit a second glance from such a high-class person as Edward Philpott.

'Erm, it's quite a long story, sir,' she stuttered nervously, knowing she couldn't tell him all the facts. He'd be disgusted and never want to speak to her again. She shifted about on the seat. Bad memories began flooding into her mind and she pushed her chair back a little, she needed her own space.

'I'm not going to eat you.'

The Other Place

'I know, sir.' She felt silly, but acknowledged she couldn't help herself. She doubted she would ever be able to have a relationship with a man. *I'll never have children of my own,* she thought. She hadn't the confidence for a relationship. What if they discovered her secret fears and phobias? She couldn't face being in a relationship with anyone knowing they might discover her secret.

Ella had always loved children; their imaginations fascinated her and since beginning her new job, she had felt a great longing to have babies of her own to love and cherish. She knew it wouldn't be possible until she could control the terror which overtook her on an almost daily basis.

She found Edward Philpott very attractive. Not just his looks but his gentle manner appealed to her, and she enjoyed his company when he visited the nursery. In fact, she suddenly realised, she looked forward to seeing him and if he didn't visit the nursery when she was there, she was very disappointed. *Can I possibly be in love with him?* she questioned herself, gazing into the fire. If she were honest with herself, she knew the answer was an emphatic *yes*, but knowing this placed her in an impossible position as she knew her feelings would never be reciprocated. *I will always love him from afar,* she told herself sadly as she saw a lifetime of loneliness stretching ahead of her.

Watching the emotions play across her face, Edward wondered what had happened to cause her such sadness and pain. 'Ella, please don't call me "sir" ever again.' His voice sounded choked even to his own ears. Stretching out his hand, he touched

The Other Place

the sleeve of her blouse. She drew back with a small gasp just as the connecting door to the schoolroom opened and two bundles of energy in the shape of Victoria and Ralph ran into the nursery.

'Ella, Ella what stories are you going to tell us today?' they asked in unison, much to her amusement. *'Just as you told Jess and Greg stories,'* a voice whispered in her head. Startled beyond measure, she quickly closed her mind to anything not of this time. She simply couldn't afford to let anything distract her from her daytime job, but the thought lingered: *Who were Jess and Greg?*

Settling the children into their favourite chairs, she asked them which story they would like to hear.

'The Magic Path into the Forest,' they shouted loudly. She smiled. Most of the children liked this particular story as the path led them on all sorts of adventures. They also enjoyed listening to other stories she told them – The Magic Cottage was another favourite, as was The Magic Smoke.

Edward quietly left the nursery, feeling very unsettled. He really wanted to get to know Ella Earnwell better and was determined to ask her out for tea at the first opportunity. Despite her being tall and statuesque, there was something vulnerable about her. There were dark secrets hidden deep within her, he knew, and he was determined to find out what they were. He wanted to run his fingers through her hair. He knew when it was released from its bun, it would cascade down her back in long silky strands. How he longed to hold and caress her in his arms. Edward fell more deeply in love with Ella each time he saw her and he was

The Other Place

certain, despite her sadness, she shared his feelings.

'Next time,' he muttered under his breath as he took his hat and coat from Polly, 'I'll be inviting you out.'

'Beg pardon, sir?' the maid asked.

'One moment, Polly, please.' He handed his hat and coat back to her and raced upstairs.

'Excuse my interrupting you, Miss Earnwell, could you spare me a moment please?'

Nervously, she made her way to join Edward Philpott. A few minutes later, he left the house with a huge smile on his face.

***

Hurrying home after the storytelling had ended, Ella prayed Amy wouldn't be late. She still felt very unsettled, but knew if she kept herself busy until her friend arrived she wouldn't dwell on negative thoughts.

Despite her worries about seeing the spirit of her stepfather, she was bubbling over with happiness that Edward Philpott had asked her out. She still couldn't believe it and wondered why a man of such high standing in the community as he was would be the remotest bit interested in her. After all, she was just a poor girl from the countryside. She certainly had no money or social standing. Try as she might, she couldn't see why he would be interested in her.

Preparing a sandwich for herself in the small kitchen just off the living room, she heard a sound.

Having left the door unlocked for her friend to

come in, she called out cheerfully, 'Take your coat off, Amy, and have a warm; it's gone really cold.' Ella was on a high after talking with Eddie Philpott that afternoon. 'Amy, I have so much news to share with you. You're never going to believe it.'

'*Yer can share it with me as well, Ella,*' her stepfather's voice sounded next to her ear.

***

Amy was having "blue fits" as she called them. Her mother had visitors for tea and had insisted she stayed until they left. They were real talkers and she despaired of them ever leaving.

'Mama,' she finally hissed, 'I promised a friend I would visit them this evening. It's after 6.30; she'll think I'm not coming.' She also wanted to pass her news on to Ella. She hadn't been able to this morning due to her friend's distress.

'Sit down at once, Amy. You can't walk out on our guests,' her mother told her.

Dismayed, she sat down on one of the sumptuous sofas in the lounge and, plumping up one of the silk embroidered cushions, she vowed she would never lead such a dull life when she got older. All of the women were older than her and all they were doing was gossiping about other people. Fixing a smile on her face, she looked around her. Fastening her smile even tighter, she beamed at the youngest matron in the room. Knowing if she kept quiet her mother would accuse her of sulking, she groaned inwardly as she made her way to the woman, who was wearing an awful pale lemon flouncy dress which made her look quite sickly.

The Other Place

People with almost white blonde hair and fair skin should certainly not wear pale lemon, she thought. Obviously it would be rude of her to say this, so she smiled sweetly as she sat beside the young matron, hoping she and the other guests would leave soon. She needed to make certain Ella was all right.

Chapter 12

It was Friday afternoon and Lily was peeping anxiously out of the front window looking for Pete, who was due to pick her up for her driving lesson; she was looking forward to seeing him.

Lily was dressed in her latest finery, a smart red suit comprised of a short straight skirt with a lovely boxy jacket edged with a black collar, beneath which she wore an expensive white silk blouse, which she was still in shock at the price she had paid for it. Lily couldn't forget she had always shopped cheaply at the Rag Market in the Bull Ring. The price she now paid for her clothes always left her reeling.

Alf never batted an eyelid when he had the bills. If she ever mentioned the prices to him, he would smile and tell her, 'You're worth every penny, my dear.'

She would think, *Why should I worry if he's not bothered?*

Her hair had been beautifully styled that morning, and she had treated herself to a facial and make-up session. Lily felt really good as she sprayed herself with the Chanel No 5 perfume Alf had bought her. She actually felt a bit guilty using it to flirt with another man, but put the thought out of her head knowing she was only having a little fun.

Glancing down, she admired her highly polished black stilettos. Pity she had to take flat-heeled shoes to slip on when she was driving. Still, Pete would get the full effect as she walked down the front steps. She grinned at the thought. She knew she looked more than good.

***

Parking outside, Pete sounded the car horn a couple of times. He'd seen Lily watching through the front window, but decided not to let on to her.

He slid across into the passenger seat and watched her walk down the steps from the corner of his eye. What a sexy woman she was. He had waited all the week for this moment, and he wasn't disappointed. She looked gorgeous and he knew she knew it. Watching her in the car mirrors, he lusted after her and knew she wanted him. Everything about this woman shouted at him that she did, but for some reason, she held back. In spite of his many affairs, Pete couldn't remember a woman he had wanted as much as Lily.

Jumping out of the car at the last minute, he went round and opened the car door. 'Your carriage awaits you, my lady.' He grinned and gave a slight bow as she elegantly slid into the driver's seat.

If only he could get her into his flat today, everything was ready for her. The champagne glasses were chilling in the fridge alongside the bottle of champagne. He'd scattered rose petals over his bed and he had even invested in brand new sheets. Pete hoped he hadn't wasted his money and also prayed it didn't look too contrived. He

The Other Place

worried he had gone a bit over the top with the rose petals. Some of the women he had entertained liked it, but he was beginning to realise Lily was different, and perhaps they weren't really what she would expect.

He turned and smiled at her. She looked more beautiful than ever today. She radiated happiness and he realised this was what he found most appealing about her; she was such a happy little soul.

Slanting a smile at him, she greeted him. 'Hello, Pete, two-hour lesson, is it?'

'I've had a cancellation, so you can have another hour as well. If you do well, we'll put you in for your test. That's if you want the extra hour?'

'Yes, please,' she said, fluttering her eyelashes at him.

He watched as she changed her shoes, thinking, *every movement she makes is wonderful.* He felt a powerful urge to pull her into his arms and spend the afternoon kissing her. Clearing his throat and settling back into his seat, he told her, 'Head into the city centre and we'll see how you do for the first hour. No speeding up the Bristol Road, either, young lady.'

Lily smirked. 'I'll tell you what, when I've passed my test I'm going to have a burn up somewhere. I want to do it just the once, it's something I've always wanted to do, just put my foot down and go.'

'Really?' he exclaimed. 'I'll come with you to make sure you're safe. I can't have you taking any risks, can I? Anyway, let's concentrate on this

The Other Place

lesson and make sure you're ready to put in for your test.'

Lily knew she was really lucky to have Pete as her instructor; he was one of the first who had taken the test to be an approved driving instructor, and had passed with flying colours.

Forty-five minutes later, he patted her arm. 'Excellent, you'll make a first-class driver, and I don't say that very often to my pupils. Now, turn right here... now left... excellent. Pull into the kerb and we'll run through some of the Highway Code.'

Suddenly, for some reason or other, it struck him – for all her flirty ways, Lily was at times uncertain of herself; her flirtations were simply a cover for her lack of self-confidence. He was relieved he had realised this before it was too late.

Lily was, to all intents and purposes, a respectable woman and he was regretting scattering those rose petals on the bed. He groaned in dismay. He wanted to ask Lily back to his flat to have a cup of coffee and a chat, nothing more. It had dawned on him during the lesson that their relationship could last for years if they didn't have an affair. This appealed to Pete more than anything as he wanted to keep her in his life for as long as he possibly could. If they had an affair, their friendship would end and he wouldn't see her again when it ended. Whatever they had between them would be lost. He dreaded the thought of not seeing this lovely little woman again. He finally realised how tacky it was to sprinkle the bed with rose petals.

For the next thirty minutes he questioned her on the Highway Code, and then, while praising her

The Other Place

skills as a driver, he suddenly blurted out, 'You look beautiful today, Lily, if you don't mind my saying. Are you going out after the lesson? Spending the extra hour with me won't make you late, will it?'

Flashing him a beaming smile, she replied, 'Thank you, Pete, no, I'm not going out. We always have a proper sit down meal on a Friday with family and friends.' Blushing, she continued, 'I do appreciate your compliment, though.' In fact, his words made her feel good. True, Alf praised her but then he was her husband. It wasn't often anyone else told her she looked nice. His words had sent tingles down her spine.

So she does have close family and friends. Pete's heart sank. *She will never be interested in me as a lover or even a friend.*

'Erm, I've left a letter in my flat, and it needs to be posted today. Would you mind if we went and picked it up?' He waited anxiously for her reply.

Chapter 13

Babs knew she couldn't live with Chrissie forever. She needed her own home. Deciding she had to be positive, she went to the council offices in Birmingham and demanded, in her most officious voice, that she be given an interview immediately. Her stomach tightened at her temerity, but she was at the end of her tether living in her sister's small flat.

'It's no joke,' she told the housing officer. 'We live cheek by jowl, you know, and I have to wash everything in the sink and dry it by the fire, there's no garden where I can hang our washing out. Sometimes I have to hang it out of the bedroom window, you know. Would you like to dry your smalls out of the bedroom window?' she didn't pause for an answer. 'It's no place to bring a youngster up. We have nowhere to put our things away. It's so crowded in that room, it's unbelievable. Three of us all living in one small room and they call it a flat. Huh.' She laid it on thick.

The officer looked at her with sympathy.

'I will see what we can do, Mrs? What's your husband's work?'

Babs hesitated, and then decided to be frank.

'Actually we're separated and I don't know where the bugger is,' she replied tersely, holding Simon tightly.

'Oh, I see,' the officer noted, peering over her glasses at the young woman.

'Right.' Shuffling her papers together, she stood up. 'We'll be in touch shortly, thank you for coming in.'

CHAPTER 14

Waiting at the bus stop, Babs had an uneasy feeling she was being stared at. This wasn't the first time she had experienced this sensation. She kept glancing round wondering who it could be. This time she caught sight of a man wearing a bowler hat and a smart coat. He was standing on the street corner, pretending to read a newspaper, but surreptitiously keeping an eye on her. Anxiety shot through her and her heart rate increased dramatically. She bit her lip nervously and wondered what to do. Fortunately there were a lot of people around and she knew whoever he was he couldn't snatch her baby or attack her. Thankfully her bus arrived, and once seated she glanced out of the window; there was no sight of the man anywhere.

Why would anyone follow me anyway? she thought. *I have a baby in tow, and I'm hardly Diana blinking Dors. Though come to think of it, I wouldn't mind her lifestyle; she has it all: looks, money, friends, everything she could possibly want. Still, I have Simon, so I suppose I'm lucky.* Although truth to tell, she felt far from lucky. *Who the devil was that man?* Thinking she had imagined him looking at her, she turned her thoughts to other matters.

The thought she might have to leave Birmingham upset her deeply, but there were no council houses to be had anywhere in the city

The Other Place

whatsoever. 'It's Alf's and Alan's fault,' she muttered darkly. Babs James (she used her maiden name whenever she could now) never thought to take any responsibility for herself; everything wrong in her life was always the fault of somebody else.

She hurried back to the tiny flat hoping against hope she hadn't been too honest with the council officer about her separation. She had to tell the truth, she argued with herself as she peeled potatoes for the soup, making sure she cut the skins off thinly as their mother had always instructed them.

'Don't you cut them skins off too thick and waste them spuds,' she'd shout at her and Chrissie as they stood at the kitchen sink preparing the family dinner.

She was so sick of these cheap meals. She was sick of living in this one room with only a view of the busy road outside. She was sick of having no money. If she could get a job, the money would help, but it wasn't worth it to her as she would have to pay a child-minder.

She knew her mother would willingly look after Simon, but Alf had stuck his oar in there and told her no way. 'She's made her bed, let her lie on it.' He'd looked really smug when he'd said it, she remembered – he was a mean pig. She dug the knife into the potato hard, digging an eye from it, secretly wishing it belonged to Alf. Anyway, why should she work? She was a mother and her son needed her.

Thinking of her mother, she realised how young, happy and smart she'd been looking of late, and wondered why. Her mom had never been scruffy, but in recent weeks there had been a subtle change in her appearance and, try as she might, Babs couldn't see a reason for it; she radiated happiness and her skin glowed. She knew Lily was taking classes in various things, but why had she acquired such a secretive air? It couldn't be to do with her driving lessons, could it?

***

Chrissie desperately wanted a change of scene. Late one night, lying in her single bed, she made plans to leave Birmingham and start an entirely new life. Babs had shocked her by saying the council had allocated her a house in a village called Edgeford near Tamworth, Staffordshire. 'It's a new housing estate they're building,' she'd told her, and went on to say she would be glad to get away from this horrid flat.

'I'm thinking of Simon,' she said, 'he deserves better than this. At least he'll have a garden to play in, and at his age the move won't upset him. I don't want to leave Birmingham, I love the city, it's me home, but we desperately need a house. I'll be back as soon as I can, though.' She hadn't a clue as to how she would achieve this, but it helped her psychologically, thinking about returning before she'd even left; it gave her hope.

Chrissie would be sorry to leave Kitty; she was very concerned about her health, but she would definitely keep in touch; she was the nicest person she had ever known.

The Other Place

More than anything, she wanted to get away from Alf Brown and his selfish ways. She knew Lily had tried to put money away to help with Simon, but Alf kept a tight hold on his finances and Lily could only slip Babs and Simon the odd pound or two. Alf paid for everything. She didn't know how her mother put up with it.

True, her mom had a certain amount of independence, insofar as she had her classes, but she had lost her financial independence. She knew Lily would miss it; when they were separated, Lily had looked after everything for years. Now, figuratively speaking, Alf held the purse strings.

Making her mind up to move home, the following day she bought the Evening Mail and scanned the 'Houses For Sale' section. She spotted an advert for a new housing development and the deposit for a house was just fifty pounds. *I can buy one of them,* she thought jubilantly. Over the years, she had been secreting pound and ten-shilling notes away in a bag. No one knew about it, but she actually had quite a lot of money saved. Deciding yes, she would buy one if she could arrange a mortgage, she took the decision to visit the village of Bridgemount in Staffordshire on Saturday.

Chrissie was also more than hopeful that once she had moved, she would lose the feeling she was being followed. At times when she was out and about, she would suddenly become aware that someone was watching her every move, particularly when she was visiting Babs or Lily. It was a horrid feeling and she found herself constantly looking over her shoulder. Why anyone would follow her,

The Other Place

she couldn't fathom. Sometimes she considered carrying a small penknife with her just in case she was attacked, but thought this was taking it a little too far. All the same, she was concerned. Strangely enough she had never mentioned this to anyone, but then the fear of being laughed at made her keep many things to herself.

***

A friend from work gave Chrissie a lift to the small country village just outside Rugeley. The housing estate was called Silver Wood, and the show garden fitted the description exactly, having silver birches in the back and front gardens. Chrissie fell in love with the house and the area immediately. She felt as if she belonged and desperately wanted to live there. If she could have, she would have stayed there and then. Everywhere was so spacious and airy; it felt wonderful after the crowded city and tiny flat.

Her friend took her into the small market town where she bought some of the local papers.

Later on, she excitedly read the job adverts to Babs.

'Gosh, this looks really good, sis, there's plenty of work over that way; you won't be far from me in Edgeford. You know what I was thinking? I can always take on extra work if my wages don't cover all my expenses.'

Nodding, Babs agreed with her. 'Don't overdo it, though.'

'It will just be until I'm settled.' Chrissie didn't

The Other Place

want to spend all her savings. She had a great fear of being poor, but there was no way she was going to have things on credit, she would rather do without. She was determined to show Alf Brown that she, Chrissie James, was someone who could be successful in her own right. Thinking about some of the things he had said to her and Babs when they were children made her shudder. Just for a second her expression darkened as the memory of a dark place came into her mind; she heard screaming and started to tremble.

Seeing her sister's expression alter and her face go pale, Babs jumped up from her seat. 'Chris, are you all right? Whatever's the matter? You look as if you've seen a ghost,' she exclaimed.

Shaking her head, Chrissie quickly reassured her sister. 'Yes, I'm fine. I just felt someone walking over my grave.' She flashed a tremulous smile. Thoughts flittered around her head like moths, and she quickly changed the subject, fearing the awful feeling of claustrophobia would take over her mind.

***

Babs was full of grandiose ideas. She wanted to fill her home with beautiful furniture just like her mother's new home; she was already looking at taking out loans and hire-purchase agreements. She reflected, *If there's a Co-op in Tamworth, I'll take out a club card account, and I'll get me dividend as well.*

'There's a council nursery not far from where I'm going to live, I'll be able to get a job and pay off any debts I run up,' she told her sister.

The Other Place

The trouble was she didn't want to leave Simon in a nursery, or anywhere for that matter, he was the most precious person in her life. She wanted to make her home a nice place to bring him up. She also wanted to impress her mom and Alf. No way did she want Alf Brown coming and turning his nose up at her new home, but work? She wouldn't leave her precious son, she would have to be desperate before *she* took a job.

'I hate where we live now. They call it a flat, but it ain't a bloody flat, it's a room and a scruffy hole. Me and Simon are going to be just fine in our new house. I'm not being rude about our flat, but oh, Chris, it's so exciting, isn't it? New lives for both of us. Who knows, you might meet someone and get married.'

Her sister shook her head vigorously. 'I'm never going to get married,' she declared. She still had a horror of being close to anyone, male or female. She didn't even like family or anyone being near her. If they did, she would begin to panic and feel threatened.

'Marriage is not for me.' Her voice held such conviction that Babs stopped knitting the jumper she was working on for Simon and looked at her with shock.

'Blimey, you sound as if you mean it, our Chris.'

'I do. I'll be independent all my life. I made my mind up years ago.'

Babs was shocked. She'd often wondered why her sister never went about with boys when she was younger, but had always put it down to her being a bit fey. She couldn't think what possible reason

The Other Place

Chrissie had for saying she wouldn't marry. Looking across at her sitting on the other side of the fireplace, she saw the closed expression on her face and decided now was definitely not the time to ask.

'I'm going after a technician's job at the local electronics factory,' she calmly informed Babs.

'Erm, right, what does a technician do, then?'

'I haven't a clue,' she laughed. 'But it says here in the Rugeley Times, training will be given. I'll enjoy it far more than working in the greengrocers.' Suddenly she chuckled. 'I haven't got very good references, have I, sis? I looked after the youngsters for Mom, then when they went to school, I went to the shop.'

'I'd say you have excellent credentials. You've shown you're reliable by helping the family out when Alf left. You've learnt good managerial skills by running the home when you were so young. Look at the skills you've learnt at the shop. You've proved again you're reliable and trustworthy; after all, you managed it for them for years. I think if they don't take you on at the factory, they'll be the losers.'

'Thanks, Babs, I never looked at it like that.' She got up and squeezed her shoulder.

'Mind me knitting,' Babs spluttered. 'I'm not very good at following patterns as it is.'

'It looks really complicated. What's it called?'

'Fair Isle, and it's very difficult using these circular needles and keeping the colours right. My goodness, it took me hours to wind the wool round the back of an old dining room chair. My arms fair

The Other Place

ached when I'd finished. I'm doing it for Simon, you know, for when he's grown up. I might not be around to knit it later.'

'What do you mean, you might not be around?' Chrissie asked worriedly.

'Nothing, you noodle.' Biting her lip, Babs could have kicked herself. Sometimes words leapt out of her mouth before she could stop them.

At times she worried she would die before she was forty, she had thought this from when she was young, but had never confided in anyone.

Chrissie gave her a puzzled look and went on to say, 'What work do you think you'll find in Tamworth, sis?'

'I'll find something,' she replied airily, 'but we need to settle in, first.' Placing her knitting in her lap for a second, she continued, 'There's an old castle in Tamworth, it's got an open-air swimming pool. What's it like where you're thinking of going?'

Chrissie's face lit up. 'It's really beautiful. The village is surrounded by countryside, it's on the edge of Cannock Chase. The whole area is so different to here; it's like being transported into another world. It's all so open and the air smells clean and fresh. I know I'm going to love living there.' She suddenly remembered the sight of the power station looming in the background of Rugeley, but shut her mind to it. Nowhere was perfect, after all.

'If my mortgage is accepted, I'll get my friend Derek to run us all over to Bridgemount, and you'll be able to see it yourself.' *Then I'll be free of the stalker,* she thought gladly.

The Other Place

'You'll love it.'

Babs doubted it very much. She wasn't really one for the country life, in fact she was dreading moving to Edgeford, which was quite countrified but at least there were some decent shops in nearby Tamworth, and a bit of night life. The trouble was the council hadn't given her any other options closer to Birmingham. *I'll move back if I hate it too much*, she told herself, *Mom will have to help me and Simon out if I arrive on her doorstep one dark night*. She smiled thinking of the black looks Alf would give her if she did – wouldn't he rant! As if she would ever ask him for help; she would live on the streets first. If only Alan hadn't let her down, but she wasn't even going to think of him. She knew he was working abroad now, and she hated him for not supporting his son. *Not that I need his rotten money*, she told herself huffily. One day soon she planned to divorce him, but this would take time and money, neither of which she had much of.

CHAPTER 15

It was a foregone conclusion Babs would hate her new home with a passion and she did right from the moment she moved in. 'It has no character,' she told her mother when she called her from the phone box down the road. 'Every other house looks the same. I hate it, Mom,' she cried, 'I just know I'll never settle here. I don't know anyone.'

'Come on, luv, pull yourself together, you have young Simon to look after. Look, I'll get Alf to bring me out to see you at the weekend. I'll bring Simon some exercise books and a bike. He'll love them. When I've passed my test I'll be able to come on my own.'

Babs' heart dropped at the thought of Alf looking down his nose at her new home.

'Leave it a few weeks, Mom.' She gave a huge sniff. 'I'm just being silly. Let me get straight first. Erm, Mom, Simon's a little young yet for those sort of presents.'

'I'll put you some money in the post instead,' Lily whispered down the phone, obviously not wanting Alf to hear her. 'As for the presents, I thought as you could keep them for when he's older, but I'll keep them for you. I have more room, after all.'

'That Alf's such a pig,' Babs grumbled under her breath, strapping Simon into his pushchair. Scurrying back home past all the identical houses on the new estate, she sighed wondering how she could have ever thought she'd be happy here. It was quite a way into Tamworth, and she had looked round the castle but ancient buildings weren't her thing. She shuddered at the idea of the open-air swimming pool in the castle grounds, swimming wasn't her thing either.

Surrounding the housing estate were fields and farm houses. She hated the countryside with a vengeance. All those green fields got on her nerves, and sometimes she could smell the cows. When this happened she had to rush home and close all the windows in case the smell drifted in. Babs James wasn't a country girl.

Carrying her baby around the empty rooms, she held him tightly. 'These rooms are like my life, apart from you, my precious.' Planting a kiss on Simon's soft cheek, she continued, 'Empty spaces everywhere, but we'll fill them up, heh? We'll walk into town tomorrow and buy some carpets and furniture, make it feel like a real home. I know I'll have to get a job at some time in the future, but I don't want to.' She clung to his small body; the truth was she didn't want to leave him in a nursery. After all, she'd never been apart from him since he'd been born. Tears swamped her eyes.

'I hate Alan and I hate Alf,' she spat the words out as if they tasted ugly and dirty in her mouth, 'both of them have let us down.' Simon, sensing her despair, started to cry. 'Don't cry, my precious.' She jiggled him up and down. 'It'll all turn out for the best. I'll get us some lovely things. I want you to have a good life and I'll always do my best for

The Other Place

you.'

'*For as long as you can,*' a voice whispered in her ear. She shivered, closing her mind to the words, and hurried to get Simon's tea ready. *No more negative thoughts*, she decided, and began to prepare a vegetable broth for her son.

***

'We'll soon be putting you in for your test,' Val, Chrissie's driving instructor, told her. Val's words gave her a huge confidence boost. So far she'd had eight lessons and was now on to double lessons; she'd spent hours learning the Highway Code.

Chrissie was thrilled at the progress she was making, and planned on buying a second-hand car when she passed her test. The bag was empty of money; since moving house, she thought it far wiser to open a bank account and let it gain interest. Since becoming a home owner, every penny had become important to her.

Reading the local paper, she spotted a company advertising for staff. It was a photography laboratory. The job description appealed to her and she decided to make enquiries. Photography would be a lot cleaner than working at the factory, and the fact they called it a laboratory spoke volumes to her. It would be far nicer to say you worked in a laboratory than a factory. If the pay was good, she would certainly be interested.

***

The Other Place

'I can't keep up with you,' Lily moaned down the telephone, 'you've changed your job already.'

Chrissie was in the phone box on the street corner opposite her home. 'Mom, I'd been at the factory for nearly two years! This job is far more interesting and it's a nice clean place to work. I love my job; it's so different to anything I've ever done before. I'll tell you all about it when I see you. It's hard to explain over the phone.'

'If it's complicated, don't bother.' Lily laughed. 'You know I'm thick.'

'Don't put yourself down, Mom, you're clever. You passed your driving test first time. I bet I don't.'

'You will, Chrissie, just concentrate and you'll get through. If you do pass, we'll be able to see more of each other. It'll save me driving all the way over to your place. We'll meet in Birmingham and go shopping together, that'll be nice.'

'Yes, Mom.' *Without Alf being there*, she thought; how she detested him.

Hearing the pips, she called before the line went dead, 'See you soon, Mom.'

Back home, she surveyed her lounge with critical eyes. It did look poor with just a few rugs scattered over the brown floor tiles. She'd bought a second-hand dining room table with four chairs – the surface was a bit scratched but she'd covered it with a lace tablecloth she'd bought at the market – and a cheap three-piece suite which she'd covered with some throws so it looked bright and cheerful. It would do for now; she refused point-blank to get into debt. *That way leads to disaster*, she repeatedly

The Other Place

told herself whenever she felt tempted to overspend. Her cheap floral curtains, purchased from the local church jumble sale, were nothing to write home about either, but they did the job. Her home had a lovely atmosphere which meant everything to Chrissie. It reminded her vaguely of Fellfeld after Alf Brown had left.

Upstairs wasn't much better, but she had a bed and blankets, what more could anyone ask for? It was hers, she owned it, and was quite proud of the fact the only money she owed was for the mortgage. *I'll pay it off as soon as I can,* she told herself repeatedly.

If she passed her test tomorrow, she was definitely going to buy a car. This wasn't a luxury; it was a necessity as it would enable her to take on more work. Chrissie James had big plans now she was a home owner.

The one thing marring her new-found happiness was that Lily had told her Kitty had died. She was very upset about it and was having a job coming to terms with her friend and mentor's death. She knew Kitty wouldn't want her to grieve, but she couldn't help it. She had loved her; she was the nicest person she had ever known.

Keeping busy had helped to keep the awful feeling of claustrophobia at bay, but she knew it could return with a vengeance at any time. She really wanted to find a solution to her problem.

The young woman needed Kitty's guidance so she could return to her past life, as the last time she had visited it, she had been upset at seeing Alf directing his evil in Ella's direction. She shuddered

The Other Place

at the memory.

Chrissie wondered, with Kitty gone, how she could possibly return to Ella's time. She needed the confidence that Kitty's presence gave her before attempting self-hypnosis alone. She had to find out exactly what had happened to cause her to lack confidence and almost destroy her life with so many fears and phobias. It would be lovely to meet up with Amy again. How wonderful it was that Amy had returned as her friend in this life when she needed her most.

Kitty had mentioned two incidents happening in her past. Obviously, one of them was what Ella had seen, Alf shutting her in the cupboard for mentioning Amy. The cruel, evil, twisted man had left her there and gone to the pub. No wonder she hated him. No wonder she suffered from a fear of enclosed places and had so many other fears. What she was having difficulty in understanding was the trapped feeling in her mind. This was terrifying, and she knew it had started quite a long time after the fear of enclosed places had happened

After a great deal of reflection, she recalled someone saying once that the one way to succeed with a bully was to show them you were stronger than them. It was so obvious when you thought about it. If she had known this when Alf had bullied her perhaps she would not have suffered so much.

Her predicament was how she could return to her other lifetime now Kitty was no longer here to guide and protect her should something go wrong.

Chapter 16

Alf was angry with Lily. He knew she had been giving money to her elder daughters and also buying things for them.

How dare she! He had worked hard for what he owned. He could only assume she had been saving money from the small allowance he gave her. How could she give them his hard-earned cash? They weren't even of his blood. Well, he would put a stop to this today, once and for all.

'Lily, a word,' he called, beckoning her to him.

'What do you want, Alf? I'm waiting for the girls to give me a ring. I thought I'd drive over to see them at the weekend.' Lily was cock-a-hoop since passing her test; she spent every spare minute in the driving seat. She liked the car Alf had given her and the allowance he gave her for petrol was more than adequate.

'I've been thinking. I'll fill your car up for you at my works over Benton way. I've got a garage there. It seems a bit stupid you spending money at the pumps when I can get it for free, so to speak.'

Lily's heart leapt in delight, *More money for the girls,* she thought gleefully.

'So you won't need the allowance I make you anymore,' he smirked.

He's so bloody mean at times, Lily fumed, wanting to smack him one. She sidled up to him and, reaching up, stroked his hair, thinking to herself

The Other Place

how thin it was getting lately. 'You always did have a lovely head of hair, Alf,' she murmured flatteringly, pushing herself sexily against him.

He shifted uncomfortably. His wife could always wield her sexual power over him.

'You mustn't stop all my allowance, Alf. What if I break down miles away from home? How will I get back? I do need money, you know.' God, Alf was meanness personified, at times he was just like Scrooge. She felt quite bitter remembering everything Alf had put her through, and now he was trying to control her just as he had when they had first married. True, she lived in luxury, but was it worth it when Alf tried to control every minute of her life? At least Pete was still in the background; she grinned at the thought. *Alf still doesn't know about him.* She was determined to keep him a secret.

She would catch herself thinking of what life would be like if she moved in with Pete. She wouldn't be nearly as wealthy but they would have fun, she was certain. But could she leave her kids and Alf? She had always thought she had loved Alf, but since meeting Pete she was changing – he was good company, and far from controlling.

Lily was beginning to realise just how wrong she had been not defending her daughter from Alf. At times she hated herself, realising that although she hadn't actually locked Chrissie in the cupboard, she was equally as guilty because she'd known about it and hadn't done a thing about it. *He's a wicked man and if I got away from him and his controlling ways, maybe I can make it up to my girls.*

The trouble was he wouldn't let Jess or Greg go

The Other Place

with her, but they were older now and would make their own decisions eventually. This was her and Pete's time... if he wanted her.

She knew Alf watched her and there was no way she could make amends with the girls with him in the picture. If she made a new life for herself with Pete it would be a start. If she could bring herself to do it. It was going to be an enormous step to take.

'What you thinking about, Lily.' Alf's voice distracted her.

Bloody hell, she thought. *I can't even think without him asking questions.*

'Nothing, love.' She kissed his ear, and he groaned thinking of what might happen later on.

'Okay, I'll give you some money every week, don't want you stranded, do we?' He scooped her up in his arms. Forget about later, he wanted her now.

'Well, Alf, this is unexpected,' she purred, unknotting his tie, happy once again at having got her own way. *I won't leave him*, she thought, snuggling her head into his shoulder; *after all, when he dies, I'll get everything. I'll be able to make it up to my girls then.* Having assuaged her conscience, Lily looked forward to her evening.

***

Later, lying beside Alf, she remembered the lesson she'd had with Pete when she had first found herself in his flat. She had thought he was trying to seduce her when she'd peeped into his

The Other Place

bedroom and seen rose petals on his bed, but he hadn't made any advances. She was glad as she didn't believe in sex outside of marriage, but she was really pleased she and Pete had become good friends; when he knew Alf was out at work, he would ring her and they sometimes met at one of the cafes in town to have coffee and cakes. It was fun, something that was sadly lacking in her life nowadays.

One or two afternoons, they had even daringly been to the pictures and, whisper it quietly, he had even kissed her once when they had sat in the double seat in the back row. He had held her hand in the theatre when they had been to the matinee of a ballet, but they both knew it was friendship and would never lead to anything more. It could quite easily have developed into a serious fling, she admitted to herself, but she didn't want to spoil what they had. Lily also enjoyed the subterfuge. This was her secret friendship that no one else knew about and she wanted to keep it to herself, away from Alf and the girls. One of the things she enjoyed more than anything was when Pete would put a 'rock and roll' record on in his flat and they would dance until they were exhausted. Then they would cuddle up beside each other on the settee with coffee and biscuits. Lily found Pete to be the perfect companion and friend.

***

Meanwhile, Pete continued to hope that one day she would fall in love with him. She was a few

The Other Place

years older than him, but looked and acted younger. She still occupied his daily and nightly thoughts even when he was in other company. There was simply nothing to dislike about Lily, and at times he was filled with jealousy towards Alf.

Pete had never married. At one time, the very thought of it would send him into blind panic. Now, however, whenever he thought of Lily, he wanted to marry her. The thought appealed to him more and more and he wondered what she would say should he ask her. He realised he truly did love her. Of late, he had begun to tire of other women. When he was with one of them, he could only think of Lily. His desire for chatting them up had left him. This was something that amazed him, but he accepted it was Lily he wanted and no one else.

He played out various scenarios in his mind where she would fall lovingly into his arms gasping, 'Yes, yes, I'll divorce Alf and be with you for eternity. I thought you would never ask.'

In another scenario, he pictured her falling about laughing at his absurdity. 'Marry you?' She would shriek with laughter. 'Give up my luxurious home for your flat?' Then she would grab her coat and go home, still laughing. He really couldn't face her scorn, it would break his heart.

Chapter 17

Finding her friend quite distraught when she let herself into her flat really upset Amy.

'Ella, tell me what happened,' she cried, sitting beside her and putting an arm protectively round her friend's shoulders.

Slowly, Ella related how her stepfather had reappeared and had asked her what Eddie Philpott had said to her. 'It was awful, just awful.'

Amy decided she needed to take control of the situation there and then. 'You have to be strong to get through this. Your stepfather is a very controlling man and knows how afraid you are of him. The more fear you show, the more likely he will try to control you. I do understand exactly how you feel and my advice is should you ever come into contact with him again, either in person or spiritually, face up to him. Another thing is, if he knows you have a strong friendship with someone, he will begin to back off.'

Ella nodded. 'I see what you mean, and think you're right.'

Stroking Ella's hand, Amy continued, 'I do know once you have someone in your life, he will disappear. You see, he would fear retribution for all he has done to you. Rest assured, Ella, I know happiness is just ahead of you.'

Ella shook her head, not fully understanding Amy's explanation. 'You mean, if I marry, he'll

The Other Place

disappear?'

'Yes, but not just that. If you have love or success of any kind in your life, he will disappear.' She smiled and put her other arm around her friend. Holding her closely, she whispered, 'Don't worry, Ella, I'll always be here for you.' Pulling away from her, she told her quietly, 'I'm going to prepare you a small snack.' Going into the tiny kitchen, she quickly prepared a tray.

'Here you are, eat some of this bread and butter, it will help steady your nerves before you go to bed. You certainly don't need anything heavier. Now, promise me you will retire as soon as I've left. Or would you prefer it if I stayed the night?' She didn't want her friend to be alone that night.

Ella was about to agree when she remembered there was only one bed.

Noticing her hesitation, Amy added, 'I can stay, Ella, Mama won't mind.' She knew her mother *would* mind but her friend's need for company was far more important. She would just have to face her mother's wrath when she returned home.

Still Ella hesitated, then realising how selfish she appeared, she flashed a quick smile. 'Thank you, I know I'm being silly, but I feel so threatened. Oh dear, I only have a single bed. I'll sleep in the chair.'

'Silly goose,' Amy declared, laughing, 'we can sleep top-to-toe, it will be fun.'

'We're of similar size so one of my nightdresses will fit you.'

Taking a spare nightdress out of the small chest of drawers, Ella handed it to her and sighed with relief, pleased her friend was staying with her. If her stepfather's image returned, Amy would be there to help her.

Ella puzzled as to how her stepfather could appear in her flat as if from nowhere. It seemed he had even materialised from another century to threaten her. She shuddered in fear and wondered how she would be able to cope, should he reappear.

She thanked her lucky stars Amy was around to help and comfort her. Her thoughts then turned to the arrangement she had made to meet up with Eddie Philpott later in the week. She couldn't believe he would be interested in her.

CHAPTER 18

Chrissie liked her new job in the photography laboratory and knew she had found the right job for her. The staff were mainly women, and what she liked was that they all had to wear white coats, it added to the general airiness and lightness of the working environment.

She enjoyed the women's company. Lunch breaks were fun. The younger girls chatted in the main about their boyfriends and nights out, but the older women, when not discussing husbands, often talked about clairvoyants and mediums. There were quite a few in the area. She enjoyed listening to them talk about their latest readings, particularly when they told each other some of the predictions they were given.

One day, one of the women started laughing. 'This woman said I was going to meet a handsome man and he would whisk me away for a week's holiday in the Lake District. Me, a married woman with four kids, I ask you. I should be so lucky.'

And won't you be surprised when it happens! thought Chrissie James, seeing an image of the man on the edge of the woman's aura.

A young woman piped up, laughing shrilly, 'One clairvoyant told me how I was going to have ten kids. That's a laugh as I've had my womb out!'

They all laughed at this and one of the women chipped in, 'Blimey O'Reilly, she was on the wrong

The Other Place

wavelength, wasn't she?'

Another day, one of the other women looked particularly glum and someone asked her what was wrong.

'It's what this medium told me last night,' she told them gloomily.

'Come on, girl, spit it out,' one of the women called, laughing raucously, 'it can't be that bad.'

'It will be if what she said comes true.'

The group of women chorused, 'What?'

'She said he's going to leave me.'

'Well,' one of them piped up, 'you've always wanted him off your hands. You're forever saying you're going to kill him. If he does leave, you'll be okay.'

The woman wiped a tear away and an awkward silence descended over the group. One of the other women went and sat beside her. Placing a comforting arm around her shoulders, she asked, 'What did she actually say, Edna?'

'She told me he'll be dead within six months if not before.'

There was a collective gasp around the room as the women looked stunned at her words.

Chrissie was horrified to think any reputable clairvoyant or medium could relay the upcoming death of a relative to a client.

Getting up from her chair, she went and sat on the other side of the woman. Offering her a tissue, she placed a comforting hand on the woman's arm.

'Edna, what the medium said to you was out of order. No one has the right to inflict such pain and distress on another person. I'm so sorry for you. It

The Other Place

was wrong of her to say such a thing.' Squeezing her arm, she continued, 'If ever you want to talk, you know I'm always here. There's nothing I can say that will take her words back, the damage is done, but you don't have to accept her words as proof positive. The best advice I can give you is to try and move on with your life and do your best to forget what she said.'

The end of break was signalled and giving Edna's arm another squeeze, Chrissie followed the women back into the laboratory.

From then on, Chrissie James became the confidante of the laboratory girls. Whenever one of them had a worry, and there were many, it was her they would ask first. Gradually, her employers began to notice how the staff approached her for advice and she was eventually offered a job as the work's staff counsellor. This was a new position created especially for her. The management team were young and forward-looking and could see the benefits she offered the company and its work force.

Thus, her reputation as a confidante and counsellor was born. Word quickly spread beyond the laboratory as the women from work told friends and relatives how brilliant she was at her job. From time to time, people would approach her outside the work environment asking for her advice. Chrissie's reputation was growing fast.

She was busy and, all in all, content with the way her life was shaping up. The main thing frustrating her was being unable to revisit her other life; she was certain she would build up her

The Other Place

confidence soon. Occasionally, late at night, the awful claustrophobia would return and leave her feeling devastated. She had to revisit the past before long.

The darkroom at the photo lab where the photographs were developed was one of Chrissie's biggest fears. Just to go near the room sent her legs to jelly; in fact, rather than walk past the door, she would take a longer route to wherever she was heading. Her fear of dark and enclosed spaces was absolute. She realised her fears and phobias were illogical, but had no idea how to recover.

Try as she might, nothing seemed to help her. She refused to take drugs. 'They mask the problem,' she told herself. She hoped that the passage of time would dim her fears.

Chapter 19

Babs wasn't faring very well at all in her home, and Lily began to despair of her eldest daughter.

'Look at everything you've bought on the knock, young lady. How the devil are you going to pay for it all?' she declared angrily when she visited her one day.

Babs looked sulkily around her nicely furnished lounge. 'Well, I can't live in a pigsty, can I, Mom?' she whined. 'You wouldn't want your only grandchild brought up poor, would you?'

'Well, it didn't do any of us any harm. You should take a page out of Chrissie's book, look how hard she works, and she's paying her mortgage off. She hasn't filled her house with things on the knock like you have. She's even got a cleaning job to help pay her way.' Pausing for breath and lighting a cigarette, Lily looked around. 'I admit, it does look nice, girl, but how are you going to pay for it?' she asked again.

'I'm starting work on Monday, Mom,' Babs told her smugly.

'Are you really, my luv?' her little face wreathed in smiles. 'You've lived here quite a long time, Simon is settled and doing well. Have you made plans for when he goes to university?'

'Give me a chance, Mom, he's still only twelve you know! One thing at a time. I have to pay off some of my debts before I can think about

The Other Place

university. My job starts late afternoon, a neighbour will keep her eye out for Simon, he's sensible for his age.' Seeing her mother frown, she added, 'I'll get more money doing the afternoon shift. I'll soon clear my debts. Oh, Mom, I know I've left getting work a long time but it seems to be the right time now to start. I didn't fancy leaving Simon when he was younger and time seems to have slipped by very fast.'

'I'm really pleased for you, luv, and Alf will be too.'

'Got nothing to do with him,' Babs snapped back, thinking what she was going through was due to his and Alan's miserliness. 'All it would have taken to help us out was a cheque from Alf or Alan for a few thousand quid and we'd have been fine. I wanted the money for Simon, not me. I wouldn't touch a penny of their money, it's tainted. Mean sods the pair of them.'

Lily restrained herself from biting back.

'Oh, our Chrissie is going to be so relieved for you, luv,' Lily trilled. 'I'm proud of you both making your way in the world.'

She blushed at her mother's words. 'I'm not exactly setting the world on fire, Mom, it's only a factory job.'

'Yes, but look what happened to Chrissie, she started in a factory, and now she's talking of setting up her own company.'

Babs jutted out her chin. 'Chrissie this and Chrissie bloody that,' she muttered under her breath.

'What did you say, pet?'

The Other Place

'Nothing, Mom, you going now?' she asked, seeing Lily holding her car keys.

'Yes, I have to get Alf's tea, and I want to avoid the rush-hour traffic. I mustn't miss Coronation Street; it's a cliff-hanger. Bye, let me know how you get on at work.'

Sinking back into the soft leather armchair, Babs chewed her lip despondently. Factory work, you could stick it for her, surely there was something else she could do? Twelve years of living here and buying things on credit had made her debts spiral out of control. She'd taken out loans to pay off some of her debt but now it was imperative she found work soon or she was in danger of being made homeless. She was less than keen to go to the factory, but had no choice.

Monday afternoon arrived and Babs nervously did her jacket up. It was cold and she felt worried at leaving Simon to his own devices, but what could she do? Her debts were catching up with her. It was Christmas in a couple of months and she would have to buy presents. Resentment flared when she thought of Alan, he could have at least set up a trust fund or given her money for their son. *Why should I have to leave my son,* she thought, *and go out to work? It just isn't right.*

Chrissie did send her money from time to time, but it was never enough. Perhaps no amount of money would ever be enough for Babs James. Any money she received normally went on food and clothes for Simon, but she always made sure she had a packet of cigarettes to take home with her. *Why not?* she would think, *I'm a good mother and work hard to keep my house clean. So why shouldn't I treat myself to a packet of fags, I deserve a treat now and then.*

For a long time she'd had the feeling she was being watched, but always convinced herself she was being paranoid; although she knew in her heart of hearts there was someone watching her, she didn't want to admit it to herself. A few cigarettes helped calm her down and keep the fear at bay. She remembered when she had lived in Birmingham, from time to time she had felt as if someone was stalking her and had even caught sight of him once at the bus stop.

Another time, quite a few years ago, she had been heading home after a shopping trip in Tamworth; Babs knew instinctively someone was following her. Nervously, she began to walk faster. Having heavy shopping bags impeded her progress, and glancing round she caught sight of a dark-haired man wearing a leather jacket and grey trousers walking not far behind her.

Panicking, she almost ran towards the bus station in the town centre. She was scared whoever it might be was going to kidnap Simon.

It was only after she had arrived home and thought about it she realised no one would want her child. There was only Alan, Simon's father, who would have the slightest interest in her baby, and as he'd never made any attempt to see him, it was highly unlikely he would try and snatch the child. She scolded herself for her irrational thoughts, but the fear was never far away.

The thought scurrying round her mind was that the man she had seen wasn't the same man she had once seen in Birmingham. She worried about this and wondered if she should tell the police. Logic prevented her from doing so as she realised she had nothing tangible to show or tell them. After all, the police needed concrete evidence not suspicions, and Babs thought she would feel really stupid telling a police officer she *thought* she had been followed on two separate occasions by two different men. The thought inched into her brain that perhaps she was watched at other times, but hadn't noticed. This caused her some disquiet and she quickly changed her train of thought.

'My trouble is,' she had told Simon recently, 'I'm on my own for far too long and I begin to imagine things. If I told Chris or Gran that someone was stalking me, they'd tell me off for being stupid.' It helped her to air her feelings aloud, but she was certain Simon thought she was imagining the sightings. She had experienced many sleepless nights worrying about who the stalker could be, and hoped he wasn't one of these madmen she read about occasionally in the paper.

***

Now payback time for the debts had arrived; pushing her umbrella up to shield herself from the wind and rain, Babs tip-tapped down the road. She couldn't remember a time when she had felt so down and out. The only thing keeping her going was her hatred of Alf and, to a lesser extent, Alan.

***

The Other Place

Waiting on the windy street corner, Babs was cold, tired, depressed, and wanted nothing more than to go home. She knew it would be a few hours yet, she had to earn some money. Her legs were freezing from her umbrella constantly dripping water onto them. On arriving at Birmingham New Street Station, she'd popped into the toilets and pulled her skirt up high. She had to admit, she looked quite snazzy: her skirt was white cotton with black laces trailing down the front, the tiny white frilly top she wore with it complimented the skirt perfectly.

All she wanted to do was to go home, she felt far too nervous for anything like this. What would her mother or Chrissie think of her if they could see her acting like a common prostitute? Which she would be if she went ahead with her plan. She shuddered in disgust at herself.

To get herself through it, she had adopted a new identity and called herself Daisy. It was the only way she could cope. She was no longer Babs, it really didn't matter what she got up to, did it?

In the station toilets she'd plastered her face with makeup, taken her blonde hair up into a pony tail and teased a few strands to hang loose. She hoped she looked sexy.

She planned on having a few tattoos done when she'd earned enough money; one in the centre of her back would look really attractive, she thought, idly tapping her foot as she waited under the street lamp.

Just then, a long sleek car drew up and the door

The Other Place

swung open. 'How much, love?' The man gave her a searching look.

He looks filthy rich, she thought. *I'm going to try my luck here. He's loaded. If he comes up trumps, he'll be my first and last punter for tonight.* 'It's a hundred quid for ten minutes.'

'Jump in,' he ordered.

Snuggling into the warmth of the car's comfortable interior, slanting her eyes at him, she offered, '£200 for thirty minutes.'

He nodded.

She shivered in apprehension. She could go home straight afterwards, she consoled herself, even if he cut up rough. Mind you, if he did, he'd feel her stilettos and she had a knife in her bag, so he'd better watch his back.

Driving along, he asked her a few questions, but she was reticent in her replies. So far she hadn't made up a full life story for Daisy.

'Hmm, you're a quiet one,' he chuckled, stopping the car on a patch of wasteland. 'At least tell me your name?'

'Daisy,' she snapped, 'and don't expect the full works for two hundred quid either.' If he coughed up she needn't go out touting for customers for a week.

Leaning across, he cupped her chin in his hands, and looking into her eyes, he told her, 'Now then, I know you're not called Daisy. Your real name is Babs, isn't it?'

***

The Other Place

Chrissie had set up her own counselling business. She had done a psychology course during the evenings and had passed with flying colours. The business was going from strength to strength. Social Services and the local probation services were so overworked they sent her clients. She enjoyed her work, but realised there was definitely something missing from her life. She had no social life whatsoever. Most evenings she studied advanced psychology and social work. In a few years time, she was definitely going to have a dog. She would be able to take it to work with her so it wouldn't be left for long periods alone; not yet, though, she was far too busy. In certain cases, she knew a dog was good therapy for some patients; stroking and talking to the animal would help them to relax and unwind.

Deciding to take a couple of hours off one day, she popped into the local library. Strolling around, she came across a section devoted to psychic phenomena. She wondered if there was a book on the shelves which might point the way to Ella and Amy's time. She was certain Ella could help her solve the mystery of her past.

A book on time-travel caught her eye. *Perhaps,* she thought, *this is what I experienced, not actually living a past life?*

The assistant who date-stamped her book remarked she had read and enjoyed the book.

'You're interested in psychic matters?' Chrissie asked.

The woman nodded. 'I'm not the only one either, this genre is very popular with the general public.'

***

Finishing the book later in the week, Chrissie realised she had definitely not time travelled. She was more convinced than ever she had led a previous existence.

She sat back and began to seriously try to recall exactly what had happened the last time she had visited Ella's time.

Settling in her comfy armchair, she tried to find the confidence to will herself back into the other time, but try as she might, she couldn't. *I'll have a cup of hot chocolate,* she decided, when suddenly she became aware Kitty was with her in spirit. She started counting backwards from ten.

***

To her shock, she found herself lying in bed and Amy's toes were poking out near her head. The thought popped into her head, 'I really am Ella.'

They were giggling fit to burst. 'I'll cover your feet up for you or you'll get cold,' she said, poking Amy's shoulder with her big toe, thus sending Amy into shrieks of laughter. Pulling the blanket over her friend's long toes sent a shudder of excitement through her as she touched her skin. *Stop it, don't be stupid,* she told herself fiercely, *she's your best friend.* Turning over carefully so as not to disturb the blankets, she asked, 'Are you comfy down there, Amy?' she knew full well she wasn't, but what else could they do?

The Other Place

'I'm fine. Tell me, Ella, who was the ghost?'

Ella shot up in bed. 'You saw him?'

'Yes, he was rushing out of your flat when I walked in.'

'Oh my goodness, I didn't realise you had seen him. Amy, he said his name was Alf, but he's identical to my stepfather Arthur.'

'You say the ghost is your stepfather Arthur, but he calls himself Alf?' Amy asked in a confused tone.

'Yes, he was dressed in different clothing, but he's identical to Arthur. Amy, I'm so afraid.' Shuddering, Ella felt tears choking her throat; she took some deep breaths, trying to control her feelings.

She shuddered again, feeling Amy's foot gently rubbing her arm. She moved as far away as she possibly could, taking further deep breaths to steady her feelings. She wanted her, but she was her best friend, her feelings were wrong, what was she going to do?

'I wonder what's happening?'

'Ella, you have to face up to him. He's a bully. In fact, he's not here in the physical form. Your *fear* of *him* is so strong it's actually bringing his spirit into your life and mind. You are acting as a channel for him.'

'My goodness,' Ella noted, amazed, 'I honestly never thought of that. Amy, you're quite right. The only trouble is, how do I overcome it?'

'If his spirit reappears, be strong, Ella, and face up to him; this will rid you of him forever. He is the worst kind of bully. Over the coming months,

The Other Place

your other fears will gradually abate. I can't promise they will disappear forever because when you are stressed, they will more than likely return. Fortunately, you know they will leave you and never ever be as bad as they have been, and as I said, if he sees you are successful, or in a loving relationship – or both! – he will disappear from your life because you will be stronger than him.'

'Thank you, Amy. You're the best friend I have ever had.'

'You're more than welcome. Now I want to hear all your other news. I know you're bursting to tell me.'

Ella giggled and told her how Eddie had invited her out and how she had arranged to meet him the following week.

Amy jumped out of bed and snuggled in beside her, the right way up this time. 'That's so wonderful for you, you can leave your awful past behind you. Eddie's love will always protect you from your evil stepfather.'

Sighing with relief, Ella relaxed and curled into her.

Amy then proceeded to tell her friend she was getting married. 'It makes no difference to the way I feel about you, Ella, I love you very much and always will. Our friendship and love will span the centuries.'

Ella nestled into the warmth of her friend's body, 'I love you, Amy. It's so good to know you'll always be part of my life.' She cupped Amy's face and kissed her passionately. Amy responded to Ella's kiss, sealing her love for her friend, she took her in her arms.

It felt so right to Ella... being held and loved by her friend. For the first time in her life she felt wanted. She believed her friend when she told her she was beautiful and that she loved her. Loving Amy was the most wonderful experience Ella had ever had.

Arthur watched the two girls from afar, he was filled with anger. By loving Ella, Amy had taken away his hold on his stepdaughter. He also realised that Edward Philpott loved Ella and would be important in her future. In the circumstances, he resolved that, as Alf, at least he had the satisfaction of knowing he had ruined his step-daughter's life. The trouble was she was doing well in her business venture; this angered him as he could no longer control her, she was too strong for him. If he wasn't careful she could ruin him.

***

Chrissie opened her eyes as memories swamped her mind like a river in full flood, of how Alf had shut her in a cupboard at the back of the house. He had done it because she had mentioned having an imaginary friend, and what was even worse, Lily knew about it. Chrissie shuddered at the memories and tears streamed down her face as she saw herself as a little girl, crying, heart-broken in the dark cupboard. She had heard Alf laughing as he slammed the door, leaving her to face the prospect of hours spent among the spiders' webs and the mice. She had cried and cried. It hadn't happened

The Other Place

once, either, he had done it several times. No wonder she had developed her fears and phobias and at times felt apathetic when she was young... what child wouldn't when they were treated in such a terrible manner? How could her mother let him abuse her? What sort of woman would let a man abuse her daughter? *My mother, obviously*, she thought. Was it fear of Alf that had prevented Lily from stopping it? She would never know now as there was no way she could challenge her.

She was glad Ella had found Amy to be such a good friend, just as she had been to her. And she hoped she would marry Eddie Philpott. *If only it would happen to me*, she thought.

'It will, my duck, just be patient,' Kitty's voice sounded comfortingly in her head, and she smiled in gratitude.

Even so, she knew Alf Brown still had the power to frighten her and she shivered at the memories of those far-off days. She hoped she would never have to see him again. Unfortunately, he was married to her mother, so she knew this was impossible.

Chrissie realised Ella had suffered abuse at the hands of her stepfather and pity welled up in her chest. *At least she got away from him. I have to find a way to overcome my problems, and then I will beat Alf at his own game once and for all.* To think he had managed to materialise in Ella's world was shocking indeed. The thought of this crystallised her intention to ensure Alf never terrorised another child again.

Wiping her eyes, she recognised she still had the other incident to overcome that Kitty had mentioned years ago, but she knew this was too big

The Other Place

for her to cope with now and she closed her mind against any more memories.

***

Babs was having coffee at Chrissie's.

'Have you noticed anything different about our mom over the last few months, Babs?'

'How do you mean, Chris?' She was sipping her coffee and smoking a cigarette.

'Well, anything different.'

For a second, Babs looked puzzled. 'Now you mention it, yes, I noticed the other week when I phoned her, she repeated things she'd told me the day before, and it's not the first time either. I've noticed it on and off this last year or so. She does seem to be getting forgetful, but doesn't everyone?'

'It's not just that, sis. When I've been out with her in her car, she's forgotten where's she's been going quite a few times. Last week we were coming home from town and landed up in Fellfeld at our old address. Another time we were going to the Bull Ring market and she forgot the way.'

'That's so scary, have you discussed it with Alf?'

'You know him, he hates talking to me, and anyway, he won't face up to anything unless he has to. Jess is away at university, he only has Mom at home, all he does is shrug his shoulders and tell me I'm daft. He's always said nasty things to me and you. I suppose we should be used to it by now.'

'What can we do?'

'I don't honestly know, but she could have an accident and kill herself or some innocent person.

The Other Place

She's not safe to drive. What upsets me is she's still comparatively young; she's only in her fifties, you know. I always thought it was like really old people who lost their memory.'

'Oh dear, but there's not a lot I can do. You know Alf hates me, Chris.'

Running her hands through her hair, Babs leant over and stubbed her cigarette out in the glass ashtray. Crossing her slim legs, she admired her fashionably short skirt, which she was wearing with the latest platform shoes. Personally, Chrissie didn't think the platform shoes or short skirt suited her sister. Her legs were far too thin to do them justice and the curly perm hairstyle she now had made her face appear too small.

Chrissie preferred wearing the latest maxi-skirt look and boots, saying, 'I'd rather hide things, especially as I'm getting a bit older. I realised some time ago if I wear anything short, it makes me look even taller.'

'You've done well for yourself, sis. This place you've bought is a big step up from the house you started off at in Bridgemount,' Babs remarked, lighting yet another cigarette with a flick of her disposable lighter. She started giggling. 'Do you remember how Mom would tear a strip off the newspaper and light it in the fire when she lit her fag? I always thought her hair was going to go up in smoke.' They both laughed.

She said, 'I remember the awful lavatory we had to use at the back-to-back house. Alf would go and sit and read his newspaper in it for an at least an hour and use all the strips of newspaper off the string. It used to stink in there something awful. Goodness knows how many cigarettes he smoked while he was in there. He had some dirty habits did Alf Brown.'

'I got into the habit of sticking some newspaper up my cardigan when I went after him in case he'd used it all.'

Chrissie added, 'Do you know, I can't imagine using newspaper now, can you? I bet the print used to rub off on our backsides.'

Wiping tears of laughter away, Babs said, 'No, I can't, and I'd hate to go back to those days even though we can now laugh at some of the things. Remember the Reckitt's blue bags Mom used for the washing, remember the blue water? She swore by it. I can just about remember using Queens Gravy Salt. Listen to me going down memory lane, you'd think I was an old woman; I'm only in my thirties! Things are so much easier nowadays, you'd think we'd have more free time, but we still seem to be busy doing other things.'

'I'm pleased you like the house, sis. I love it. It's Victorian, you know, like Mom's in Kings Heath. I was glad when they moved from there to the other side of Fellfeld, it's a lot easier to visit her now, isn't it? Mind you, their new one is twice the size of this as it's two knocked into one.' She sighed. 'I've always liked it, it's atmospheric; mind you, so's mine.' Confidentially, she leant forward, breathing quietly, 'This house is haunted, you know.'

Babs squirmed back in her chair, tucking her legs under her. 'You've seen a ghost?' She gazed around nervously. She never felt comfortable when

The Other Place

discussions turned to ghosts or anything to do with the paranormal. After all, what if one of the spirits told her sister about her? She'd die of embarrassment if she or her mother found out about her secret life.

'I've seen more than one in this house,' Chrissie informed her sibling seriously. 'I was vacuuming around the fireplace when suddenly a young street urchin appeared in front of me. Of course, I nearly jumped out of my skin with shock. He was wearing a cap and it looked as if he had chopped at his hair with a knife. He had a very dirty face, but a really cheeky grin. His ragged shirt was hanging out of his equally ragged pants. I knew he was from the Victorian era.'

'Did you speak to him?'

'No, he disappeared in an instant. I hope I see him again.'

'Tell me about the others.'

'This is a strange one. I was walking through the kitchen the other day when I saw a short, plump woman standing at the sink. She looked as if she was washing the pots. She had huge arms and was wearing a large white apron and white mob cap. Her hair was dark brown and curls were springing out from around the cap. She didn't see me at first, and I stood watching her. I heard her humming a tune I'd never heard before. I don't know what made her aware of me, but she glanced over her shoulder and smiled and winked at me! Then she said the strangest thing.'

'What?'

'She said, "I'm from the other house in the city.

The Other Place

The missus sent me over to clean up."'

'Oh my goodness, that's so strange. What happened then?'

'I gasped and she vanished as if she'd never been there. Can you believe it, Babs? I kept thinking about it and asked Linda, she's a work colleague and knows more about ghosts than I do.'

'What did she say?'

'She said ghosts are known to return to a place where, say, they have been happy or unhappy, or it could have been a special anniversary. Linda said there isn't always a specific reason for us seeing a ghost. It could be our spirit guides bringing them to us, simply to prove there are ghosts.'

'Yes, that makes sense.'

Looking at her, Chrissie asked, 'You feeling all right, sis?'

'Yes, why?'

'Oh, I just thought you looked as if you'd lost a bit of weight, and,' peering closely at her, she added, 'you look a bit pale. Are you eating all right?'

'Yes, of course I am. Stop fussing, for goodness sake. You know I hate it.'

'I wish I could lose weight, I've always been on the large size and I don't suppose I'll ever be slim,' Chrissie sighed. 'You, Mom and Jessica got the looks and figure; I don't know what happened when God painted my face. I think he must have been having a bad day. He built me a bit like a carthorse as well.' She laughed self-consciously, shrugging her broad shoulders. 'I don't even look like you. I must take after our father, and never having seen him or ever likely to, I'll never know.

Not that I ever want to see him, what he did to Mom was unforgivable.'

'Ermm.' Babs flushed she seemed uncertain what to say. 'Chrissie, you're not ugly; you're different to us, yes, but you're far from ugly. You have beautiful eyes and gorgeous thick hair. I envy you; it's such a lovely honey blonde. Believe me, you are beautiful. Maybe our father had his reasons for not contacting us, who knows?'

'What makes you say that? Do you know something I don't?'

'Of course not, you silly devil. How would I know anything about him? I was just speculating. Have you ever researched the history of this house?'

'Blimey, nothing like changing the subject, is there?' Chrissie laughed. 'Erm, I haven't, why?'

'It might be interesting.'

Nodding slowly, she smiled. 'You're so right. I should have done it before, but it's one of those things you do when you're older and have more time. I always seem to be in a rush.'

'I'm not as daft as I look, you know.'

'Why on earth do you think you're daft? That's a very strange thing to say, completely out of the blue. You're not daft at all, you're a clever woman. You should believe in yourself more. You have so much more confidence than I have.'

'Me, more confident than you, who has her own home and business? Get away with you, sis, have you lost the plot or something?'

'But it's all a front. I'm fine at work, but inside I lack confidence in many ways.' Feeling this was all

The Other Place

getting far too personal, she changed the subject. 'There's something I've always wanted to ask you, but if you would rather not talk about it, don't worry.'

'Ask away, I can always say no.'

'Have you ever felt as if you were being stalked? I'll tell you why I'm asking; I used to feel as if I was being watched, particularly when I came to visit you or Mom. It was a horrid feeling. The feeling disappeared about twelve years after you moved Tamworth way. All very peculiar'

'Erm, no, our Chrissie.' Flushing again, she added, 'I never have.'

Chrissie knew instinctively Babs was being lax with the truth, but she didn't pursue it. She was more worried by her sister's apparent lack of energy and general look of ill health.

'I'll make us a cup of coffee, and then I have a story to share with you. I think it's about time you heard it.'

Making the frothy coffee in her espresso machine, she wondered what had led her to tell Babs she would share her secret with her.

***

'Blimey, sis,' Babs gasped in astonishment after Chrissie had detailed her life as Ella. 'I can't believe you went through all this and never told me anything about it. I'm really shocked. You really believe you lived before? What era did you see yourself living in?'

Chrissie nodded, her hair falling across her eyes.

'Yes, I know I did. I was Ella. Is it so impossible to believe we have lived other lives, and we will live again in the future? I know this is going to sound very strange, but I saw myself living between times. Do you remember the imaginary friend I had when I was a youngster?'

Her sister nodded.

'Well, believe it or not she was my friend in the other time.' Chrissie decided not to mention the relationship she had with Amy. It had been so beautiful she thought telling Babs would somehow spoil it.

Babs gazed round-eyed at her sister. 'Never! Well that's incredible, so she actually lived another life as well. You think we come back then, as someone else, not as ourselves, and we can live in any period even in-between times? This is all very strange and hard to take in.'

'Yes, I've thought about it a lot and Ella's time didn't fit any particular era, and I know there are lives we live between times, as there are also parallel worlds. Lets talk about it later when we have more time, and,' glancing at her sister, 'when you're feeling a bit better.'

Tears welled up in her eyes. 'So, Mom might return as someone else's mom after she dies, and when we die and come back, we won't be sisters. Chris, that must have been awful for you to see Alf in another time. I can understand how scared you must have been. But then it wasn't really you, was it?' Brushing the tears away with the back of her hand, she gave a huge sniff.

Chrissie said, 'Yes, but it wasn't as if he could

The Other Place

physically hurt me, was it? I was scared, but I've since realised a number of things about him and I've finally got his measure.

'Now, stop worrying, neither of us is going to die for years and years, I don't think we should be thinking about it, do you?'

'But what if –' she tried to interject, but Chrissie shook her head.

'Let's not talk about it now, when we make it personal it gets depressing.'

'Chris, how can you say that when you've just been talking about leading a past life?'

'Yes, but that was then, this is now, and I don't want to talk about any of us dying. I enjoy talking about these things, but nothing too close to home, otherwise it gets miserable.'

Sighing, Babs agreed.

Chrissie could see Babs wanted to talk about spiritual matters so suggested they held a small séance.

'Erm, no.' She really didn't want to risk her sister finding out about her life. Not yet, there was plenty of time to talk in the future.

'What about a card reading?'

'Chris, I'm really only interested in reincarnation.'

Her sister groaned. 'Okay, Babs. You win, let's go to the library and see if there are any books about it. They'll be able to explain it far better than I can. Just remember, though, the writer is only putting forward *their* point of view.'

Babs gave a huge grin and slowly got up from her chair. She was anxious to go and investigate the books and find out all she could. If only she didn't feel so tired and ill, she knew she would enjoy the research more.

CHAPTER 20

That Alf wouldn't answer the telephone left Chrissie distraught. She was lonely, utterly lost and totally bereft; having no family support at this shocking time in her life was unbearable. Never having made any close friends, she found herself out on a limb. There was no one in the world she could confide in. At one time she had seriously considered calling the Samaritans, but how could they help? They couldn't bring her mom back.

Remembering how quickly Lily had died was terrible. The dementia had developed rapidly and she been taken into a nursing home. It was horrible seeing their mom degenerate into someone they couldn't recognise as their bright bubbly mom. Lily had the best possible medical care available, but nothing helped. Towards the end, she hardly recognised anyone at all.

Chrissie would never forget the shocking telephone call. It was the nursing home to say Lily was dangerously ill and had been rushed into hospital. Chrissie telephoned Babs and then went to the hospital, but they were too late. Their mom had died of pneumonia before they arrived.

She was devastated, now she had only Babs as her last full-blood link to her mom. She discounted Alf and her stepbrother and stepsister, as over the years they had distanced themselves from her and Babs. She actually had the strong impression they disliked her and Babs. They never sent birthday or Christmas cards, never telephoned or wrote to either of them. If Lily invited them to Alf's house, which they never called home, their brother and sister were noticeable by their absence.

Discussing this one day with Babs at her home, they had both agreed how alone they felt. Their aunts and uncles hadn't contacted them during Lily's illness. It was as if they were embarrassed by the mumbling person their mom had become.

If anything, Lily's death seemed to hit Babs even harder than Chrissie, and she had spent hours comforting her the following day. She had done her best to console and counsel her. Babs was utterly distraught and she was really concerned about her. She knew she had to put her own grief on hold for the time being and help Babs through this awful time.

Two days after Lily's death, the telephone had rung. She automatically thought it was Babs seeking comfort. To Chrissie's utter disbelief, it was the hospital urging her to get there as quickly as possible. Her sister was in a critical condition after being involved in a car accident.

To her and everyone else's absolute disbelief, Babs died. Chrissie was grief stricken and didn't know how she would survive. She seriously thought about committing suicide. Darkness enveloped her, and at times she did not know whether it was night or day. How could fate have allowed this to happen? She functioned on automatic pilot, it was the only way she coped in the immediate aftermath of the tragedies.

The Other Place

She later found out that the driver had said Babs had walked off the pavement with her head bowed, straight in front of his car. He simply couldn't avoid hitting her. Chrissie thought her sister's grief had led to her being careless as she crossed the road and this had led to her death.

Chrissie was beside herself with grief and didn't think she could take anymore. All she did was cry, she didn't sleep for days, she was heartbroken and bereft; it took all her strength to arrange the funeral. This was the only time she spoke to Alf as the family had decided to hold a double funeral.

Despite everything, Chrissie couldn't accept that the two most important people in her life were dead. She had no one of her own blood to turn to and was in despair at what had happened. Nothing could have prepared her for the shock of Lily's sudden death, but to lose Babs in such horrific circumstances had left her in anguish.

Eventually, she had no tears left, and drawing on all her remaining reserves, she realised she had to be strong for the funeral. Her family deserved the best she could manage.

She knew it would be the hardest day of her life; *and then what?* she thought. Suddenly, a glimmer of hope shone through the gloom: there was Simon, who she adored; she could help guide him along the way. She would probably never truly get over the loss of her mother and sister, but she knew in the fullness of time, she would continue to help others through her work.

Feeling just a little better, Chrissie decided now was the right time for her to have the dog she had promised herself all those years ago, it would bring some much needed company and comfort into her life. She could take her new friend to work with her at a later date. This was the first step on the long road to recovery. She looked in the telephone directory for the local dogs' home.

***

Stroking Ben later that evening, Chrissie felt comforted by the feel of his soft black fur. Ben was a two-year-old mongrel and he was beautiful. He had followed her trustingly to her car from the dogs' home. Love shone from his beautiful soft brown eyes and he didn't want to leave her side. She didn't want him to either. 'It's just you and me now, Ben,' she confided, brushing his shiny coat. For no reason, she glanced up and whispered, 'Thanks for Ben, Babs.'

'It's okay, sis,' her sibling's voice trilled through the lounge. Ben's ears twitched as he looked around for the owner of the voice.

'You heard her, didn't you, Ben? Babs, where are you, sis? Talk to me, please.'

There was no reply, but Chrissie was certain she was near.

Going upstairs, she took one of Lily's jumpers and one of Bab's blouses out of the airing cupboard. She had found the jumper in with Bab's clothes and brought it home, along with Bab's other possessions.

She inhaled their familiar scents; it was the closest she could get to them now they had gone.

The Other Place

Memories of her mom and sister returned, flooding her mind and heart. Tears flowed in abundance. How would she ever accept that she would never see them again? At times she wished she had died instead of being left to endure the endless lonely days and nights.

***

Lying awake, Chrissie wondered how Ella and Amy were faring and started counting backwards from ten.

***

Ella glanced nervously around her. She was a few minutes early for her meeting with Eddie. She hoped she looked suitably dressed to be going out with such a well-presented young man.

Amy had dressed her hair for her and insisted she borrow one of her outfits.

Knowing she really didn't own anything good enough to go out to a smart restaurant, she had agreed to her friend's generosity.

Seeing her reflection in the mirror, Ella couldn't believe the person staring back at her was really her. Amy had brushed her hair until it gleamed.

Her jacket and skirt were made of dark green velvet to match the ribbon holding her ringlets high on her head. She wore a blouse of cream silk with a ruched front and high neck. Her black court shoes peeped enticingly out from beneath her skirt. The small bag she clasped in front of her also belonged

The Other Place

to Amy, as did the beautiful gold earrings and chain. The one thing bothering her was the corset Amy had insisted she wore. It was so tight; she found it difficult to breathe.

***

'If only I could hold this precious day forever,' glancing around for Edward.

She was a little nervous about the street urchins running up and down the road, but the doorman was keeping a wary eye out for them.

The street was filthy, and a horrible smell lingered on the air. The shopkeepers were still busy plying their wares and litter was strewn around. Horse traffic and various delivery drivers were out looking for extra trade. She knew the cleaners would be out in the early hours and she pitied them as she did the young children who had to work to bring in extra coppers.

People were milling around everywhere, some not so well-off, looking as if a good meal wouldn't come amiss. Beggars dressed in rags looked pityingly at the people passing by, holding out their hands asking for a penny or two. Match-girl sellers and pedlars were calling out their wares, hoping to make a few pennies. She felt so sorry for an old lady shuffling along pushing an old pram full to overflowing with rags, it was obviously all she owned in the world. It was a depressing sight. She thanked her lucky stars she had found well-paid employment.

The doorman approached and invited her to sit

in the foyer while she waited for her companion. Relieved to be inside, she relaxed as she waited for Edward.

After a meal in the luxurious Maylen restaurant, Eddie suddenly surprised her by reaching out across the table and taking her hand. She thought how small her hand felt within his, as she had always been embarrassed by how large her hands and feet were. Her grandmother had told her not to be ridiculous, as with her being so tall, she would look really daft with tiny hands and feet! Laughing, she had to agree.

'Ella, will you marry me?'

She was dumbstruck – had she actually heard him ask her to marry him? He reached into his pocket and took out a small black box. He showed her a diamond engagement ring and slipped it on her finger. She was engaged and he was whispering words of love to her across the table and still she hadn't said a word.

She couldn't speak. Never in all her life had she thought any man, let alone Edward Philpott, would ask her to marry him. Never had she thought any man would tell her he loved her.

'Edward, you don't know me,' she murmured softly, looking at the beautiful diamond cluster which made up the engagement ring.

'The first time I saw you, I realised you were the woman I had been waiting for all my life.' Squeezing her hand tightly, he told her, 'If I could have, I would have whisked you away there and then and spent the rest of my life holding you in my arms and kissing your beautiful face. You are

The Other Place

the woman I want to spend the rest of my life and eternity with.' He stroked her hand gently and she felt her body tingle. His words set her senses on fire, and gazing into his brown eyes she saw how much he truly loved her. She simply couldn't believe this was happening to her and felt as if she was the luckiest woman alive.

Chrissie stirred in her sleep, but found she was being pulled further into Ella's future.

She had married Edward Philpott and looked radiant, smiling happily, surrounded by family and friends, standing outside a small church, chatting and laughing to each other. Chrissie was certain Ella would never be tormented by bad memories again. She was happy things had worked out for her.

She glanced at Ella and for a second; green eyes met green eyes across time. Ella smiled radiantly at her, bridging the centuries separating them. In an instant, Chrissie saw Ella's future open up before her: she saw her children, Katy, Johnny, Sarah and Albert, crowded around a mother they adored, and who in turn adored and treasured them. For a second, Chrissie envied her happiness, but Ella's eyes implored her not to. 'Your happiness is just ahead of you,' she whispered through time. 'Do not despair, things will turn out right. Be patient a little while longer.'

Chrissie awoke as dawn was breaking; she gazed around her room wondering how she would ever achieve such happiness after what had happened to her. After all, it was the funeral tomorrow, and she couldn't stem the rising tide of grief that again threatened to engulf her.

Kitty's voice sounded in her thoughts, 'I told you, girl, there is someone out there for you, don't give up now. This bad time will pass eventually.'

Chrissie shook her head. Recalling Kitty's words actually made her smile for the first time in what seemed like forever.

As if anyone would be ever fancy her! *Look at the size of me,* she thought, *as if any man would ever want me.* She was too tall, too big, her voice was too deep. In fact, as far as Chrissie was concerned, there was nothing attractive about her whatsoever.

It would be nice to have a close friend, but with all her different hang ups, who would ever want her? Chrissie was perpetually questioning herself and it drove her mad. *Constant introspection is bad for you,* she would tell herself, but she still did it.

At times, she would list all her different phobias, or as she now called them, hang-ups. After writing them down and reading them, she would ask herself what could possibly have caused them. In fact, seeing the long list, she knew she had to do something to rid herself of them once and for all. If only she knew how.

The thing puzzling her more than anything was seeing herself leading another life. In the beginning it had disturbed her greatly, in particular meeting Amy! But gradually she had begun to accept it had actually happened as everything was so real, and she was certain Ella's life would help her in this lifetime.

Lying back in bed, sad memories flooded her mind as she wondered what was going to happen

The Other Place

to her in the future.

'It will have to be work and more work, Ben.' Reaching down, she stroked the dog's silky ears, and other memories began to return.

Long-buried memories she didn't want to remember rose to the surface. Memories of Alf shutting her in the cupboard under the stairs for hours on end, and finally, the other incident came into her mind. She was fourteen again, feeling the man's hand across her mouth as he dragged her into the coal house and assaulted her while Lily was out chatting to her friends. The awful memories screamed in her head because the man had been Alf and he had left Lily later the same day. He had been drinking at lunchtime with his mates and hadn't returned for the afternoon shift. Finding her sitting on the doorstep had angered him and he had gone berserk. How long she lay in the coal house after the assault, she didn't know, but eventually she had managed to crawl back to the doorstep and wait for her family to return. Fear of discovery had made him leave.

Instinct had told her Lily would disbelieve her. She had felt terribly ashamed, as if what had happened was all her fault. She had shut the incidents from her mind; they were too hard to cope with.

She groaned in despair. Hearing her, Ben got up and nuzzled her face, as if to say, *'Don't worry, I'm here for you and always will be.'*

Alf had wrecked her life. What he had done to her as a child had led her to suffer claustrophobia. It had worsened after he had assaulted her, and the

The Other Place

subsequent phobias had resulted from it. As if being shut in the cupboard when she was a small child wasn't bad enough, being assaulted physically by a man who was supposed to care for her was a million times worse. At times, these feelings were so bad she had wanted to die to find peace.

At the time, it had been too shocking to remember what had happened, the memories had been locked away; the door was wide open now, and everything had tumbled out into the daylight.

She realised that by closing her mind to the incidents, she had inadvertently started the chain of events that led to the feeling of being completely trapped inside her mind. This, in turn, had led to other fears and phobias developing, giving her an outlet to be able to cope with the stress.

She decided to take control of her life. She lined her phobias up like soldiers in a straight line and ticked them off, as she now knew exactly why they had happened. They were her defence mechanism against the fear that haunted her night and day.

No wonder she couldn't bear anyone walking behind her, Alf grabbing her from behind was what had started it. Her fear of the dark and being shut in was another direct result of Alf's inhumanity. She couldn't tolerate anything being near her face, even her hair obscuring her face would set off a panic attack. The more she mentally ticked off her list, the clearer it became to her. No wonder she had felt so trapped. Alf Brown had so much to answer for.

How was she going to leave this behind her and start again? Amy's words telling her to face Alf

The Other Place

once and for all came back to her and she wondered if this would stop it. She thought it might and the thought he would never attack another child in this lifetime or in any future life made her think long and hard that this was the only way forward. If she didn't do it, she would regret it for ever more.

Calling Ben, she decided to take him for a long walk thinking the fresh air might help her to get her life in perspective.

Chrissie found solace as she strolled across the fields around Blithfield Reservoir. She was able to think through her problems and marshal her thoughts; with Ben trotting beside her, she felt hugely comforted. As she wound her way around the water's edge, the grasses whispered stories to her of times gone by. Her imagination took hold as she watched the birds drifting high across the water. In her mind's eye she saw an old mill on the bank of the River Blythe and a thatched cottage in the valley. She knew if she went and looked, she would see the foundations of an ancient mill and the old brick wall surrounding it. How different it had been in those far off days, she thought.

She thought back to another strange occurrence which had happened when she and Ben had visited a lake at Rocester. She had drifted off to sleep and suddenly found herself in Ella's flat, talking about seeing black swans on the lake. It had been a truly amazing experience, as when she opened her eyes Amy was sitting beside her, and a flock of black swans had skimmed across the lake. It was a sight she would long hold in her memory.

The Other Place

Later on, she thought, *Once the funeral is over, I might be able to move forward.* She dreaded it but knew it was something she had to go through.

***

The worst day of her life was as bad as Chrissie expected it to be. Her work colleagues helped her through it. They were more than kind, but nothing could stem the panic she felt when she remembered she would never see or hear from her dearest relatives again. How was she going to live through the years ahead without seeing or hearing them again? She swallowed hard, almost choking on the sobs threatening to spill over in a never-ending stream.

How was she going to cope with the loneliness of the years ahead? No Babs, no Mom. *How cruel life is,* she reflected, clutching her prayer book so tight it bent between her fingers. If there really was a god, how come he'd taken away the most precious people in her life? *Why would any god do this to me?* she questioned. The word, 'Why' reverberated around her brain, blocking out everything until she suddenly became aware that people were waiting for her to lead the way out of the church.

She had missed the service, blocked it out completely, unable to cope with the trauma. Everything was a blank to her until she was leaving the churchyard, when she noticed a tall, dark-haired, rugged, handsome-looking man hurrying down the path towards her.

He shook her hand, saying with tears in his

eyes, 'You're Chrissie, you don't know me but Lily was a wonderful friend to me. I'm so sorry she died, and for your sister. What a tragic time this is.' He became overwhelmed with emotion and unable to speak. Wiping his eyes with the back of his hand, he hurried off and she watched as he got into a car with a sign on the top, "Pete's Driving School".

What a nice man he seemed to be, thought Chrissie; she was pleased he had been her mother's friend.

Simon approached her and she had to smile; despite the warmth of the day he was wearing the Fair Isle sweater Babs had started knitting all those years ago. Her words returned to haunt her. 'I'm doing it for Simon for when he's grown up, I might not be around to knit it later.'

Had Babs known she was going to die? Remembering her words, Chrissie was convinced she had.

She refused all invitations to return to other people's homes. She wanted to go home and remember Babs and her mother in her own way. Chrissie didn't believe in getting together after a funeral. *Good luck to those who do,* she thought, it wasn't for her.

Sighing with relief, she closed her front door and sank to her knees, hugging and stroking Ben. He had helped to transform her life. Ben was her best friend. He would never judge her. All Ben wanted was love and affection. This was something Chrissie had in abundance.

***

The Other Place

She took many months off work. It was the worst time of her life. Night merged into day and sometimes she didn't know what day of the week it was, let alone the month. Before having Ben, she couldn't even be bothered to get dressed but since having him, she had to make the extra effort to take him out walking and she had gradually begun to feel the benefits.

She had thought seriously of closing her business. She simply could not face work, it was Dawn her PA who persuaded her not to.

Dawn engaged a temporary manager in her absence. Chrissie could see from all the reports that he was excellent at the job, but she had never spoken to or met him. Regular contact by telephone with Dawn reassured her the company was in good hands.

Gradually, life began to readjust itself and one day, whilst walking Ben in the countryside, she noticed for the first time in many months the sun was shining. Since the catastrophe, so many days had been dark and dismal, but slowly she became aware of her beautiful surroundings; the cow parsley was blowing on the wind, the buttercups were vying with the daisies, it was almost as if they were saying, 'Look at me, look at me,' as they danced on the breeze. Forget-me-nots pushed against the tall grass saying, 'Notice me.' Ladybirds floated across beautiful clusters of lady's smock. Spring lambs were growing tall and bouncing their way across the fields, calling for their mothers, skipping and gambolling with the sheer joy of being alive.

The Other Place

Walking through a bluebell wood, she drank in the magical scene surrounding her and her heart lifted. She caught the delicate scent of some late-flowering wood anemones. 'Woodland ghosts,' she murmured. Never had she seen such a beautiful scene as the sun broke through, illuminating the bluebells to a purple hue as it slanted through the silver birches; it was as if the massed flowers were saying, 'Welcome back, Chrissie.' Leaving the woods, she was met with the exquisite sight of drifts of cow parsley covering a bank that led down to a stream of crystal-clear water. Tears stung the backs of her eyes, but she walked on, thankful she had discovered this place that offered her such beauty and tranquillity.

'It's so wonderful,' she sighed to Ben. Sadness touched her, knowing Babs and Lily would never get the opportunity to see this scene. Then she grinned, imagining them chorusing, 'Give us the shops any day, you can keep your countryside.' She giggled thinking how true that was.

She had found many of her phobias had left her since acquiring Ben, and reliving the memories of what had happened to her had helped her life return to a more even keel.

Chrissie had resolved not to be a victim any longer. From what she had heard, Alf Brown's life was falling apart. Since Lily's death he had begun drinking heavily and rarely left his house. Rumours were spreading fast that his business interests were in trouble.

When she had started her business, she had ensured that her office was large and airy, with door windows she could fling wide on nice days. The main office was also open-plan. No way could she have worked in a confined space. Perhaps now things might become easier for her. Thinking of work, she knew it was time she took up the reins of her company again. Common sense told her, the longer she left it to return, the worse it would be for her.

Taking some deep breaths, she decided now was the time to take the first step back into her working life.

***

She parked in her reserved space outside the company building and felt her managerial cloak slip into place. It was as if - when she got out of her car outside the company premises - a different Chrissie emerged. A person who knew what she was doing, who had authority but overwhelming compassion for the clients sent to them from all over the county.

She was at work and nothing about her private life could intrude. This is what had helped make her so successful at her job: the ability to focus on the task in hand.

Now, Chrissie James, she told herself, *you are the manager of this counselling service and are back to fight another day.*

'Morning all,' she called, walking into the main office.

'Chrissie, what a lovely surprise, it's so good to see you.' Dawn gave her a huge hug as the rest of

The Other Place

the staff called out their greetings.

The door suddenly swung open and a deep voice called, 'Morning all.'

Turning, she looked into the deepest, bluest eyes she'd ever seen. Something stirred in her mind; it was as if she knew this man – had she met him before? She was certain she would have remembered him if she had, but why the recognition?

'Morning, can I help you?' he asked.

'Who are you?'

'I'm the manager of this company and I haven't time for chit-chat this morning. We're full to overflowing. My PA will make you an appointment. If you will excuse me, I must get back to my office.' He strode off.

Dawn was biting her lip seeing the expression on her boss's face.

'He's a bit of a livewire is our Dan, the temporary manager who's doing your job.' She giggled. 'He hasn't a clue who you are, Chrissie.'

'His PA. His office. Well, really, we'll see about that.' She marched out of the office and down the corridor, followed closely by Ben, who had been solemnly watching everything quietly. Flinging her office door wide open, she opened her mouth to tell Dan exactly what she thought, but pulled up short. The man of action was sitting at her desk with his head in his hands. He hadn't even noticed her entrance. She quietly closed the door.

***

The Other Place

'What's wrong?'

At first he was hesitant to speak, but with a little gentle probing...

'My wife left me, my home is being repossessed in a couple of days, and I'll be out of a job when you return to work.' Looking at her, his deep blue eyes clouded with emotion.

'Mm, I see you have problems.'

He raised his eyebrows. 'Just a few.'

'Nothing's that bad,' she started to say, then hesitated; yes, it was – she knew better than anyone what it was like when your world fell apart.

'Is there no one you can go and stay with for a while?'

'No. I have no family whatsoever.'

She didn't try and force him to discuss his life. She was racking her brains to see if there was a practical solution.

'I'll see you tomorrow.'

Well done, Chrissie James, is that the best you can come up with? she thought as she drove home. *Call yourself a professional counsellor and you couldn't even help the poor man in his hour of need.* Whatever was wrong with her? *Maybe it was those blue eyes?*

***

Later, sitting at home, she was perplexed. Dan, the temporary manager, certainly had huge problems, and she was uncertain how to help him. Deciding to think about it later, her mind drifted back to Babs, and she remembered Simon had given her a box filled with many of Bab's personal possessions to keep. She went upstairs and began looking through them. Picking up a book, she was surprised when she saw what it was.

It was Babs' journal! Was she strong enough to read it? She thought she owed it to her sister to try.

BAB'S JOURNAL

I feel so ill today, but I have to go to work, I need the money. Lots of expenses coming up, Christmas presents to buy, bills to pay. Simon needs new clothes. Everything is so expensive. Life is very difficult. Alf could have helped me out. I told him my problem in confidence, and he more or less said tough and told me he had an appointment. I can't tell Mom or Chrissie, it wouldn't be fair to worry them, but I'm so tired all the time. Since Dad died I've had to find work... we need the money.

***

Chrissie gasped. Why hadn't Babs told her she was ill? She was devastated to think her sister hadn't mentioned it to her. She would have been there for her every step of the way.

To think she'd actually told Alf she was ill and he'd refused to help her. She couldn't believe the callousness of the man. Why ask him and not her?

Who was this 'Dad' person Babs had mentioned?

She read on.

The Other Place

***

I couldn't go anywhere today. I just slept. I'll have to go back to the doc's. He'll adjust my medication. I can't let Chrissie or Mom down by asking for their help. I have to do my best for Simon, after all, I had him, and I've never regretted it, but I went against Mom's advice.

If I can find a way to get him to university, I will. Once he graduates, he'll have a good career.

***

You idiot, Babs. Why didn't you ask me for help? Tears clouded her eyes. *My poor, foolish sister struggling on when she was ill. I would have helped her. To think she asked Alf for help, and he refused. What a wicked, evil man he is.*

***

Simon's not going to university, he's told me he's looking for a job in Birmingham. I'm disappointed but it's his choice, I've never dictated to him. I had enough of that with Alf Brown.

This blood disorder is making me so tired. I wish the doctors could tell me exactly what's wrong with me. They're hopeful I'll recover.

The Other Place

***

God, this was almost too hard to read. She reached out her hands, she wanted to touch her sister, speak to her, confide sisterly thoughts, see her face, hear her voice and give her a hug. Even if she was still moaning about Alf, and she had good reason to, it wouldn't matter as long as she was here. How she missed her.

She continued reading.

***

I've begun to feel better. The doctors confirmed I have pernicious anaemia. They have me on the right treatment now. It's taken a while but I'm recovering slowly. I'm still getting morbid thoughts that I'm going to die. I don't understand it. I'm recovering, so why I have these thoughts I don't know. But then I've always known I'll never reach old age.

At least Simon has a job; he's training to be an electrician. What a comfort it is knowing he'll be secure once he's finished training.

***

Chrissie was heartbroken and couldn't accept her sister had not told her she was so ill. *Why,* she wondered, *why didn't she tell me, her best friend? I would have done everything in my power to help her.* She felt angry thinking that if Babs hadn't been so weak, she might not have been involved in the accident.

'You idiot, Babs,' she called to the four walls. 'Why didn't you tell me you were so ill?'

Each hospital visit Babs made mentioned that "Dad" gave her a lift and held her hand. Dad?

Who was Babs on about?

Chrissie wrapped a cloak of despair around her and cried and cried. If only she had known her sister had been so ill. She would never understand why she hadn't told her. How could she keep something so important a secret?

Chapter 21

Despite Dan's problems, she had been adamant that he remove his things immediately into the General Office. Calling him into *her* office the following day, she found him no nearer to finding a solution to his housing problem.

'You can come and stay in my spare room.' The words were out before she could stop them.

'Pardon?'

'Here's my address, pop round after work and we'll discuss the arrangements, if you want to.' With a nod of her head, she dismissed him.

Whatever had made her say that? What was the matter with her? Didn't she have enough troubles without taking in a lodger? She was still in mourning for her family and needed time to re-adjust to work. She was thinking of taking revenge on her stepfather. Didn't she have enough on her plate? Had she truly lost her senses these last few days, she asked herself?

What's more, what if the awful feeling happened to her in the night, and she screamed aloud in fear? He might hear her. How would she explain it away? What a fool she was.

***

'Are you sure you don't mind my sharing your home?' Dan asked her that evening as they sat in

The Other Place

her lounge drinking coffee.

'No, not at all, I'll get you a key cut,' she replied, certain she could just imagine what Babs would have said to her. How could she be taking in a lodger? She, who had always professed not to like men, was now inviting an incredibly good-looking man to live in her home.

'I'll start looking for work as soon as I move in,' Dan told her.

'Good, and to help you along I'll give you the names of some companies you can apply to. I'm sure you'll find a job very soon.'

The sound of something hitting the kitchen floor had them rushing into the kitchen. 'Strange,' she muttered; the cutlery drawer was open and a knife and fork were lying on the floor.

'You must have ghosts or poltergeists,' Dan laughed, bending down to retrieve the cutlery.

'You could be right, there.'

'You believe in ghosts?'

'Yes, I take it you do?'

'I didn't, but after losing my family, I have always felt as if they are with me.' His blue eyes clouded with memories again, and she could see how much pain he was in.

Chrissie suddenly saw a group of people surrounding him and realised she was seeing his spirit family. Quickly, before she lost the link, she described the older man and woman and two younger women who were with him.

He grinned when she finished describing them to him, overjoyed; he wanted to hug her, but some instinct told him to keep his distance from this

The Other Place

beautiful woman. He was aware she wouldn't welcome his or anyone else's touch.

'We were fated to meet,' he told her, his voice choking. 'Thank you for bringing my family to me.'

***

Dan settled in quickly and visited the job centre frequently, trying to find work. Unfortunately, he had found it impossible, and after a few weeks he began to feel desperate at being unemployed. He helped Chrissie by doing the shopping and any jobs that needed doing around the home, joking he was becoming a house husband. This gave her an idea. She thought a new challenge was the right way forward for her, it might help her move on, and Dan seemed an ideal candidate to assist her. Plus, she wanted to keep him near her as she was growing more attached to him by the day.

'Dan, how would you feel about helping me set up a new company?'

His eyes sparkled with interest. 'Doing what?'

'I thought we could form a company of househelpers, employing men and women to help around the home. It might be more successful than the usual cleaning companies which only employ women.' He went to interrupt, but she silenced him with a shake of her head.

'Let me finish. My thoughts are that women do the day-to-day jobs extremely well, but a househelper man can do those extra jobs that women can't always manage.'

'Such as?'

The Other Place

'Putting up hooks, wiring plugs, jobs around the garden, nothing too heavy or time-consuming like decorating, or carpentry. I don't mean fixing cars, either.' She laughed seeing his relieved expression.

'A good idea,' he laughed. 'I only know where to put the fuel, oil and water in a car. I see your point and I think it's a brilliant idea. You're right, there are a hundred and one jobs a man can do around the home a woman can't do, particularly older clients.'

She smiled, pleased he agreed with her. 'I'm sure we'll have many more ideas along the way,' she said, pushing her heavy hair from her eyes.

Dan thought Chrissie had wonderful hair and was often tempted to run his fingers through it, though he sensed her reticence and restrained himself. After all, he'd not long separated from his wife and didn't think it would be wise to get involved with someone else so soon. He felt a great empathy towards Chrissie, as he was as alone in the world as she was. He knew it would be wrong to make any advances towards her. He sensed what she needed at the moment was friendship more than anything.

Working on this new business venture would hopefully bring them closer together.

'I'm excellent at marketing and designing, which will help. What are we going to do for staff? Are you going to do the interviewing?' He didn't like the thought of her being alone with strange men. Then he realised how ridiculous he was being. Chrissie was a free agent and he had no right to be possessive or jealous. But he was, she was constantly in his thoughts and he knew he was in love and did not want to lose her.

Pleased Dan was interested in the new business, Chrissie spent many hours with him setting it up. She felt it was going to be successful. Her counselling business was growing by the day, and she was proud of her achievement. All in all, her business life was looking good.

On an emotional level, she was still deeply upset at losing her mother and sister. She had no need to take revenge on Alf Brown, fate had taken care of him; he was killing himself with drink. To her relief she felt she could begin to leave him behind.

***

Grabbing a blouse belonging to Babs from the airing cupboard, she went and lay on her bed. Holding it close to her, tears welled up in her eyes.

She still couldn't believe she had lost her mother and sister. She missed them so much; if she were honest she missed Babs the most, she had always been there for her. She was having difficulty in accepting what Lily had done, insofar as letting Alf lock her in the cupboard. Why hadn't she left him? But beneath her anger Chrissie still cherished her mom, it was like a physical ache deep inside her. Knowing she would never see or hear her or her sister ever again was too awful to think about. She had read more of the journal the previous evening and discovered the answers to her question and had found a certain comfort within its pages.

The Other Place

BAB'S JOURNAL

Last night, I went to Birmingham. I've decided to work as a prostitute; I desperately need the money to pay the bills and buy Simon's clothes.

A man driving a sleek, expensive-looking car stopped and picked me up from a street corner. I was so frightened, what if he attacked or killed me? Who would look after Simon then?

The man parked up and began talking to me. He put his arm around me, I was so scared he might harm me, but he started speaking and gave me the shock of my life!

He told me my name and everything that had happened to me since I was a little girl. He went on to tell me about Mom and Alf and about Chrissie. In fact, he knew about all our lives. The biggest shock of all was when told me he was mine and Chrissie's blood-father. For the first time in my life I was speechless.

He said he had employed private detectives to find out where we lived. Our father had then kept tabs on the three of us throughout the following years. He had seen my wedding reported in the Birmingham Mail and he knew about Simon and the different places we had all lived.

It felt weird, spooky almost, sitting next to my own father, and have him relate all

The Other Place

this to me. I must say, I felt quite sad to think that he had been unable to share our lives and had spent all those years on the outside looking in.

He told me he had written to Mom a few times asking for visiting rights, but she had ignored his letters. That shows how hurt she was at his defection and I don't blame her. I try to imagine at times how she must have felt having a young child and being pregnant with another and having her husband deserting her. It must have been horrendous for the poor woman and doesn't bear thinking about. She was only young herself and she never sank to prostitution, did she? I'm so ashamed at what I was going to do.

I felt so cheap and shoddy, but he put his arm round me and said from now on, he was going to take care of me and Simon. I told him no. I was emphatic about it, but he insisted. He drove me home and said he would visit me the weekend when we would talk.

In the house, I found he had put some money in my bag. I still felt uncertain about him, but in another way I was comforted to think he had cared enough to watch us all our lives and he had been here for me when I need him the most.

When we met up the following weekend, he told me he wanted to be a proper dad and help, so I didn't have to work. I was touched by his kindness; he wants to make up for the past. He told me he had often wanted to approach me and talk, but feared I would reject him.

***

Chrissie wiped tears from her eyes. If only she had known about Bab's financial worries, she would have helped her and Simon as much as she could.

Flicking through the pages, she had discovered how their real father had taken Babs under his wing, and thought how extraordinary it was that fate had stepped in right at the crucial moment and prevented her from selling her body.

***

So that's who it was, Chrissie reflected, *all those times I thought I was being stalked, and it turned out to be my own father or one of his private detectives watching to make sure we came to no harm.* Recalling the woman with the horse teeth who had visited the house in Brook Land, she thought, *It was a sign he cared for us, but I was too young to understand it at the time.* She realised Babs would have told him not to get in touch with her, as she had always disliked what he'd done to Lily. In fact she had said numerous times she never wanted to see him. Now she would always wonder what he looked and sounded like. A twinge of regret shot through her, but in a way it was her own fault.

The Other Place

'Well, you always said as you didn't want to meet him, you stubborn devil,' Bab's voice laughed through the mists of time.

Chrissie nearly dropped the journal in surprise.

'I wish you wouldn't do that, Babs,' she muttered.

'Well, you look like him, Chris, he was tall and you have exactly the same colour eyes and hair as him. He wanted to meet you but you always said you hated him, didn't you? He was scared you would reject him if he had sought you out.'

Ben was cocking his head to one side and looking quizzically behind his owner; he could obviously see her sister.

Quickly she turned, and was just in time to see her sister's smiling face disappear. Wiping a tear away, she cuddled Ben, thanking him for showing her where she was. So now she knew she had looked like her father, another question answered.

She admitted to herself that if Babs had asked her to meet with him she would have refused. She had always hated the way he had abandoned Lily, leaving her with Babs and abandoning her when she was pregnant. She did admire him for doing the right thing by Babs.

Making a coffee and giving Ben a bone to chew on, she thought about the journal.

From reading it, it seemed to her their father had been quite comfortably off and had given Babs money every month to ensure she didn't have to work.

He had been there for her until he had suddenly died a few months before Babs got killed. How

The Other Place

awful that she had to find work even though Alf had known about her illness. The way her stepfather had treated her was shocking.

***

'Chrissie, shall we take Ben for a walk?' Dan called.

'Good idea, I'm on my way,' she said, and leaving her sister's blouse on her bed, she hurried downstairs.

The longer she knew Dan the more she liked and trusted him. Not so long ago, she would have laughed if anyone had suggested she would eventually share her home with a man.

To her surprise, she was enjoying his company and knew if he left, she would miss him.

She no longer felt afraid when she went to bed; the terrible feeling had left her. Dan's presence in her home was a life-changing experience for Chrissie and she revelled in his companionship.

Grabbing her jacket and Ben's lead, she joined Dan and Ben, who were patiently waiting in the hall for her. Dan suggested they visit a place that not many people knew about. 'It's where a convent once stood, Chrissie, and it's such a peaceful area. For some reason or other, I've always called it "The Other Place", don't ask me why as I haven't a clue. I do know you'll love it.'

When Dan said, "The Other Place", Chrissie, tried to remember where she had heard the name before, but try as she might she simply couldn't remember.

The Other Place

***

Walking across the frost-covered grass with Dan, she exclaimed, 'I didn't even know this place existed. Mind you, we usually go to Blithfield for our walks with Ben, don't we? You've always lived here so you know it better than I do. I agree, it certainly is a beautiful place.'

The sun was just rising behind a cluster of trees. Despite the cold, she suddenly felt the magic of the morning; it seeped into her and she felt as if it touched her soul. Everywhere was touched by the sun's rays; the trees sparkled as the sun rose higher in the sky, and a light frost shimmered across the fields. Ben was running around having the time of his life barking with glee.

Suddenly, she thought, *This is "The Other Place" Kitty mentioned to me when I lived at Fellfeld. This is the place I visited in my dreams*; she recalled her happiness as a child when she had seen it in her mind's eye.

'Chrissie, I love you. Will you marry me?'

Dan's question startled her out of her reverie. She blinked in astonishment. 'What did you say?'

'Marry me, Chris, and make me the happiest man in the world.'

'But you're not divorced. Have you forgotten?'

'It will be finalised within a few months. Please, Chrissie, I love you so much, you're the best thing that's ever happened to me.'

Nothing had prepared her for Dan's proposal; in fact she had never expected to ever receive a proposal of marriage. Apart from... Kitty's words

The Other Place

drifted through her mind. 'I know you say you will never marry. You will, you know, but not until you are older and more settled. The proposal will surprise you and it will happen at "The Other Place". I know you won't believe me, but my words will return to you when it happens.'

Chrissie felt as if Kitty was actually speaking to her and thought how wonderful it was her friend had known all those years ago that this would happen to her.

Shocked by Dan's proposal, she gazed around at the beautiful wintry scene; the sun was breaking through the mist, bathing everywhere in a stunning light. She thought how lucky she was to have come through such a bad time, and Dan's love and friendship meant everything to her. The question was, did she love him? The answer was, she didn't know, as she had never experienced love before.

Would she miss him if he didn't live with her? 'Yes,' was the immediate answer, she didn't know how she could ever face an empty house again.

Did they get on well together? Again, the answer was unequivocally, 'Yes.'

Would she like to live with him for the rest of her life? 'Yes, yes, yes.'

'Well, then,' her mother's and Babs' voices chorused loudly in her head, 'you love him, you stupid bloody woman. Marry him before he runs off.'

Looking into Dan's handsome, and at the moment, very worried face, she answered, 'Yes, I will be honoured to marry you, Dan.'

His face shining with happiness, he grabbed

Chrissie around the waist and kissed her passionately.

She could hear Ben barking at the pheasants across the field; despite the frost beneath her feet, she had never felt so warm and contented in her life. So this was love, nothing else mattered in her life now apart from Dan and Ben. If only this moment could go on forever, she would be the happiest woman in the world.

***

Chrissie sat on her doorstep watching her two daughters skip down the garden path. Cassie was seven years of age, blue eyes and blonde hair. She was a happy child with a sense of her own identity. No one would ever get the better of her. Karen Ann, her youngest daughter, was five years old, green eyes, honey-blonde hair; she was a quiet, reserved child. Chrissie knew she would go far.

She knew Babs and her mother would have been proud of her and adored her family if they had lived, and she felt sad they would never play a part in their lives. Chrissie made certain she talked about them to her girls often and showed them photographs.

Surrounded by love, her phobias were well and truly in the background, and she blessed the day she had met Kitty, who had set her on the road to recovery. Her guidance and wise words were still with her even after all these years.

After marrying Dan, her life had gone from strength to strength and she realised Alf Brown no

The Other Place

longer had any power over her at all.

Alf Brown had lost everything, his business was wiped out, he had no friends or family, his children having deserted him. He was dying a sad and lonely death from alcohol poisoning in a Birmingham hospital.

Greg lived down south but she rarely heard from him or Jessica. She knew Jessica had married and hoped she would be happy.

Chrissie often looked back to her poor beginnings in the back-to-back house at Brook Land and then the move to Fellfeld. At times, she was so happy she wondered if her life as Ella had been a dream, but watching her two girls, who so resembled her and Babs, she wondered if it really mattered whether it had been or not. The most important thing was she had managed to put the trauma behind her, and if the ghosts of the past had helped to achieve this, then she was more than grateful.

Karen Ann had an imaginary friend called Katy. Chrissie often overheard her telling Katy stories about Rufus the magic cat, which could disappear and reappear at will. She thought her daughter had Ella's gift of storytelling.

One day, Chrissie was busy cooking the dinner, while Karen Ann was entertaining Katy at the kitchen table.

Suddenly she stood transfixed in shock as she heard her daughter say, 'I have a new story to tell you today, Katy, it's called "The Other Place". It's the story of two ladies called Ella and Amy who lived a long time ago.'

The Other Place

Printed in Great Britain
by Amazon.co.uk, Ltd.,
Marston Gate.